# THE MOURNES WALKS

PADDY DILLON is a prolific outdoor writer, with over sixty guidebooks to his name, including a dozen covering Ireland. He has written for several outdoor magazines, newspapers and periodicals, and has contributed to radio and digital media. Paddy has produced numerous booklets and brochures for Irish tourism organisations, and has an extensive picture library covering the Irish landscape. He has led walks around Europe, and has walked in Nepal, Tibet, Korea and the Rocky Mountains of the United States and Canada.

# THE MOURNES WALKS

## Paddy Dillon

THE O'BRIEN PRESS
DUBLIN

This edition first published in 2015 by The O'Brien Press Ltd,
12 Terenure Road East, Rathgar, Dublin 6, Ireland.
Tel: +353 1 4923333; Fax: +353 1 4922777
Email: books@obrien.ie
Website: www.obrien.ie
Originally published in 2000 by The O'Brien Press Ltd.
Reprinted 2004. Revised 2009.
Reprinted 2010.

ISBN: 978-1-84717-761-2

1  3  5  7  6  4  2
15  17  19  20  18  16

Maps: EastWest Mapping
Layout and design: The O'Brien Press Ltd
Illustrations: Aileen Caffrey
Illustrations pp.10, 101: Patrick McAfee, from *Irish Stone Walls*
Cover photograph: Paddy Dillon

Printed and bound by CPI Group (UK) Ltd, Croydon, CR0 4YY

# CONTENTS

*Introduction* 6

*1 Warrenpoint and Rostrevor* – Easy *18*

*2 Slieve Martin and Knockshee* – Moderate / Difficult *22*

*3 Slieve Roe from Knockbarragh* – Moderate *27*

*4 Slieve Roosley from Leitrim Lodge* – Moderate *31*

*5 Tievedockaragh and Rocky Mountain* – Moderate / Difficult *34*

*6 Hen, Cock, Pigeon and Eagle Mountain* – Difficult *38*

*7 Eagle Mountain and Finlieve* – Moderate / Difficult *43*

*8 Slievemoughanmore from Attical* – Moderate *48*

*9 Slieve Muck and Pigeon Rock Mountain* – Moderate / Difficult *53*

*10 The Spelga Dam Circuit* – Difficult *57*

*11 The Silent Valley Circuit* – Difficult *62*

*12 Slieve Binnian from the Annalong Valley* – Difficult *68*

*13 Annalong Valley and Rocky Mountain* – Moderate / Difficult *74*

*14 Chimney Rock Mountain* – Moderate / Difficult *79*

*15 The Mourne Coastal Path* – Easy / Moderate *83*

*16 The Brandy Pad from East to West* – Moderate *87*

*17 Slieve Meelbeg and Slieve Meelmore* – Moderate / Difficult *91*

*18 Slieve Bearnagh from Trassey* – Difficult *95*

*19 Slieve Commedagh from Trassey* – Difficult *99*

*20 Slieve Commedagh from Newcastle* – Difficult *103*

*21 Slieve Donard from Newcastle* – Difficult *108*

*22 Tollymore Forest Park* – Easy *114*

*23 Murlough National Nature Reserve* – Easy *118*

*24 The Castlewellan Loanans* – Easy *122*

*25 Castlewellan Forest Park* – Easy *127*

*26 The Windy Gap and Legananny* – Easy *131*

*27 Slieve Croob from Finnis* – Moderate *135*

*28 The Mourne Wall Walk* – Difficult *138*

*29 Ulster Way – Newry to Rostrevor* – Easy *146*

*30 Mourne Way – Rostrevor to Ott Track* – Moderate *150*

*31 Mourne Way – Ott Track to Newcastle* – Moderate *154*

*32 Lecale Way – Newcastle to Clough* – Easy *158*

# Introduction

'*Where the Mountains of Mourne sweep down to the sea.*'
Percy French.

They sweep down to the sea: that is what they say about the Mountains of Mourne. They've been saying it ever since Percy French wrote a poignant song of an emigrant pining for his native land. They sweep down to the sea at Newcastle and Rostrevor, and rise inland in huge, heathery humps. They look formidable, yet the Mournes are a very compact range of mountains. A tough walker could traverse them in a day, while an enquiring walker could spend years trying to get to know them throughout the changing seasons. This guidebook offers a selection of walking routes, from the coast to the highest peaks, allowing you to explore and appreciate this special place. The routes lie within the Mourne Area of Outstanding Natural Beauty, which embraces not only the Mountains of Mourne, but also Slieve Croob and the south Down coast.

## GEOLOGY

The Mournes are usually described as being composed of granite, but this is an over-simplification. The most ancient bedrock in the area is Silurian strata, over 400 million years old. Beds of rock were originally laid down in horizontal layers on the seabed, slowly building up into thick sandstones, mudstones and shales. These layers were later tilted and warped by a series of earth movements. Other layers of rock were deposited on top of them, including sandstones and limestones, but these have long since been eroded, and you would need to travel well beyond the Mournes to find any evidence of them.

The next significant event in the evolution of the Mournes occurred some sixty million years ago, when a massive batholith, or mound, of molten granite rose up through the Earth's crust, forcing the ancient Silurian strata into a dome. The tremendous heat and pressure resulting from this emplacement baked and altered the rocks in contact with the granite, metamorphosing them into slaty strata. More volcanic rock was subsequently squeezed into cracks in both the granite and the surrounding Silurian rocks forming minor dykes.

Within the last million years came the Ice Age. An ice cap covered the Mournes, and glaciers scoured out deep U-shaped valleys, leaving smooth slopes of granite in some places and masses of bouldery detritus in others. What today's walker sees are the domed granite mountains of the Mournes, much affected by glacial erosion, with ancient low-lying Silurian strata surrounding them, largely buried beneath a layer of glacial rubble known as boulder clay. (Walkers with an interest in geology should carry a copy of the 1:50,000 scale Mourne Mountains geological map, published by the Institute of Geological Sciences.)

## EARLY HISTORY

Ireland's earliest settlers were coastal hunter-gatherers. Evidence of Neolithic settlements has been found on the Murlough Dunes near Newcastle, in the shadow of the Mourne Mountains, and the famous Legananny Dolmen near Slieve Croob in County Down dates back over 5000 years. A later wave of Bronze Age settlers cut their way into the great forests that covered Ireland and left substantial stone structures and burial chambers. Little is known about the rituals and beliefs of these early settlers, but they did have a reverence for high places. There are ancient cairns on some of the Mourne summits, obviously intended to be seen from lower ground. On the lower ground, usually on low hills or mounds, there are still traces of ring forts and raths, fortified farmsteads with earthen banks and wooden palisades, used by extended families. Historical details are sparse and archaeologists can give us only a glimpse of these early Mourne folk.

However, with the aid of oral and written history, some bizarre events can be gleaned from the last 2000 years. The highest peak was once known as Sliabh Slainge, after Slanga, son of Partholan, who came to Ireland after the Battle of Troy. When Slanga died he was buried on the summit of the mountain. The Mournes used to be called Beanna Boirche, named after Boirche, a Celtic chieftain and cowherd. Boirche ruled his territory from Slieve Binnian in a time when a man's wealth was measured in terms of how many cattle he possessed. The Christianisation of the Mournes left another layer of folklore. St Patrick threw his sandal between the streams of Srupatrick and Cassy Water, marking the boundaries of the Kingdom of Mourne. Twelve miles it flew, measuring the 'Twelve Miles of Mourne', and of course those were the long 'Irish' miles. St Patrick had little to do with the Mournes afterwards, and it was his disciple, St Domangard, who continued the good work, building an oratory on top of Sliabh Slainge. The mountain then became known as Sliabh Domangard, which has since become shortened to Slieve Donard. St Bronagh was associated with the Rostrevor area, and a ruined church dedicated to her can be seen near the village. A bronze bell used by St Bronagh over a thousand years ago has been preserved in the more recent Roman Catholic church. A number of ancient church sites can also be visited in the area.

The territory around the Mountains of Mourne was for centuries under the control of the Magennis clan. The clan chiefs were inaugurated at a 'coronation stone' that is preserved on a housing estate on the Bridle Loaning above Warrenpoint. The Magennises were from time to time put under pressure by Anglo-Norman settlers, who constructed small castles around the Mournes during the thirteenth century. The Magennises managed to occupy the Anglo-Norman Dundrum Castle during the fourteenth century. After the Rebellion of 1641, however, the Magennis lands were forfeit and before long the whole of Ulster was systematically planted with a new influx of Scottish and English settlers.

Walkers with an interest in the history and heritage of the Mountains of Mourne should make a point of visiting the small museums and heritage centres throughout the area. Some of these are mentioned in the walk descriptions, but for more detailed information contact the tourist offices listed at the end of this introduction.

## LATER HISTORY

Looking at the Mountains of Mourne from a farming perspective, it is evident that a huge amount of back-breaking work went into clearing boulders from the boulder clay to make fertile fields. The number of boulders lifted from the ground in some places was immense, and what better way to dispose of them than to build dry stone walls? Thus were created the intricate field systems of the Kingdom of Mourne, where every field has a name and the fields outnumber the inhabitants. In the past century the small farming 'clachans', small huddles of cottages and farm buildings, were commonplace, but now the size of the holdings has increased and some old farmhouses lie in ruins, supplanted by new housing. This was once primarily cattle country, but now sheep are the mainstay of the hill farms. Cattle are still grazed in some of the lower pastures, and indeed some fields succumb to the plough and are capable of raising good cereal and root crops.

The tough granite that makes up so much of the Mournes has long been used as a building material. Boulders from the ground, from riverbeds or from the shore have been used for building purposes. It was unusual for any serious attempts to be made to fashion the stone before the eighteenth and nineteenth centuries, when stone-splitting techniques were developed using 'plug and feather' tools. Square setts, often mistakenly called cobbles when laid on roads, and long kerbstones were most easily fashioned, and the durability of the stone led to much of it being used in the building of monuments. Quarries tended to be small in scale, serviced by carts over a network of rough tracks. Today's walkers can not only make use of these old tracks, but can also find stones on the mountainsides showing evidence of craftsmanship, lying alongside little quarry faces and tumbled stone cabins. The Mournes once rang to the sound of hammers and chisels.

Many of the buildings in nearby towns date only from the eighteenth and nineteenth centuries, and some, such as Warrenpoint and Newcastle, were primarily fashioned as seaside resorts.

## WATER CATCHMENT

In the High Mournes, the attention of all visitors eventually focuses on the Silent Valley and Ben Crom Reservoirs. As long ago as 1678, the Belfast Water Commissioners were looking for a plentiful supply of clean water, and in due course they identified the Mountains of Mourne as the best source. In order to safeguard it for future use, 3,645 hectares (9,000 acres) of the High Mournes were purchased, and the Belfast Water Act of 1893 led to the construction of a vast water storage scheme that took almost half a century to complete. The project was tackled in stages: First, water from the Kilkeel and Annalong rivers was piped to a reservoir near Carryduff. Second, a vast dam was built across the Silent Valley between 1923 and 1933. There was a plan to dam the Annalong Valley too, but geological conditions were unsuitable, so, between 1949 and 1952, the Slieve Binnian Tunnel was cut to divert water from the Annalong Valley to the Silent Valley. The third and final part of the scheme involved building another dam to create the Ben Crom Reservoir, with construction lasting from 1954 to 1957.

## THE MOURNE WALL

In the early stages of the vast water catchment scheme, the 3,645-hectare (9,000 acre) holding was completely encircled by a continuous dry stone wall measuring 22 miles (35 kilometres). The men who worked on this project knew it as the 'back ditch of Mourne', but most people know it as the Mourne Wall. Construction spanned the years from 1904 to 1922, creating a monumental structure quite unlike anything else in Ireland. Although some stretches of the wall are haphazard in terms of construction, other parts display true craftsmanship and are as solid now as the day they were built. The only mortar used on the wall was in the construction of three stone lookout towers – on Slieve Meelmore, Slieve Commedagh and Slieve Donard. The 'classic' stretch of the Mourne Wall, about half its length, is from Carn Mountain to Long Seefin, with gaps occurring only where cliff faces interrupt its course. The Mourne Wall across Slieve Binnian, Slievenaglogh and Slieve Muck is less well ordered, often relying on the contorted Silurian bedrock for its substance, rather than the more durable, blocky Mourne granite. The men who built the wall used only the rock that was readily to hand, one reason why the land close to the wall is easier to walk across than the rocky slopes further away. In many places you can see where rocks used in the wall were split, using 'plug and feather' tools. On the best

Plug-and-feather tools, used for splitting rocks.

sections of the wall you can see a foundation of enormous 'footing' stones at its base. The wall was constructed by building two dry stone walls leaning in on each other, with massive 'through' stones binding the two faces together. Broad 'cam' stones laid along the top of the wall project outwards, making it difficult for sheep or people to climb over it. That was the intention: to keep people and livestock out, and you can still see rusting signs on the three lookout towers proclaiming 'Trespassers Will Be Prosecuted'. In fact, with the advances in the science of water purification, people and livestock can both be accommodated in the catchment area today.

The construction of the Mourne Wall has probably done more to open up the Mountains of Mourne to walkers than anything else. It is an obvious feature to follow in almost any weather as it runs like a roller coaster from peak to peak. In the days when the Mourne Wall Walk was an annual event it once attracted some 4000 people in a single day to follow its course. It is a monument to the men who built it, and walkers should treat it with respect.

## FLORA & FAUNA

The Mountains of Mourne have a thin, peaty soil that is poor in minerals, and a damp climate that has encouraged the growth of blanket bog. While the bogs in the Mournes aren't as deep or extensive as in most other mountain ranges in Ireland, they are nevertheless significant. Expect to find sodden areas of sphagnum moss, bog asphodel, bog myrtle, rushes, sedges and tussocky grass. Heather is widespread on the drier areas, flushing purple in summer, along with locally abundant bilberry and patches of invasive bracken. On higher ground you will find crowberry interlaced with the heather. Take the time to look carefully in the cracks and crevices on the rocky tors and bouldery slopes, as you can find some surprises in places. There are tiny saxifrages, roseroot and gnarled dwarf juniper and willow cowering in places where the nibbling sheep cannot reach.

The bird life of the Mournes is sparse, but ravens are commonplace among the mountain fastnesses, nesting in some of the most inaccessible cliffs. Their '*pruck-pruck*' call and aerial acrobatics make them easy to distinguish. Buzzards are seen from time to time gliding on broad wings, and peregrine falcons can also be spotted. Eagles were last recorded in the nineteenth century, but were ruthlessly eliminated from the face of Ireland. The most commonly seen small bird is likely to be the wheatear or meadow pipit, and it is always worth looking along the lengths of mountain streams for the white-bibbed dipper. In the depths of winter there is always room for a surprise, like the sudden appearance of snow bunting. While the mountain lakes will sometimes attract migrating waterfowl, most of the time they appear desolate. Grouse are occasionally to be seen in the heather, but their presence is often unnoticeable until they break noisily from cover, crying '*go-back, go-back*'. Catching a glimpse of a hare in the mountains is uncommon, but they are present. Frogs can be abundant at times, and lizards are more common than you might imagine.

It is around the fringes of the mountains that the species count really begins to rise. Hooded crows and magpies are commonly seen around farms and fields, with kestrels hovering by day and owls preying at night. Hedgerows make excellent wildlife habitats and, when laden with berries from hawthorns and brambles, offer great foraging opportunities for birds. Lowland lakes and ponds attract a greater range of ducks and waterfowl, and the forests have enough tree species to provide roosts and food for a great variety of birds. There are shy fallow deer in the forests, seldom seen due to their superb camouflage. The forests at Tollymore and Castlewellan are especially rich in tree species, long-established trees from earlier plantings as well as specially nurtured arboreta. In the older parts of the forests you can find a variety of fungi on the dark forest floor, but where a little light breaks through you can expect to find carpets of wood sorrel. After clear-felling in the forests, plants such as rosebay willowherb are quick

Feral goats, with their long horns and shaggy coats, may be spotted in the mountain heights.

to dominate and provide a blaze of purple in the summer. With a little patience foxes, rabbits and badgers can be spotted, and the elusive pine marten has also been recorded.

The coastal margins of the Mournes provide yet another important habitat. The Murlough National Nature Reserve is especially rich in flowery grasslands and wooded areas, attracting a range of birds. The sheltered mudflats around Dundrum Inner Bay are an important wintering ground for Brent geese and plenty of other species. Seals are commonly spotted with their heads bobbing above the waves, but will seldom venture ashore, preferring the security of isolated rocks. Cormorants often use the same rocks as they hang their wings to dry. A good illustrated field guide, such as those published by Collins, will prove an invaluable companion on these walks.

## ACCESS & WALKING OPPORTUNITIES

For the past century, walkers have been in the habit of using the Mountains of Mourne for exercise and recreation. Access on foot has generally been along quite well-defined farm and quarry tracks, some of which are now equipped with car parks. However, not all access routes have necessarily been formally designated as rights of way, even if they do have car parks and signposts. It is important for walkers to remember that they are crossing someone's land, and to respect the work that takes place in the countryside. Once free of the intricate field systems and lower farmlands, walkers have traditionally enjoyed virtually unlimited access to the mountain heights. With all rights, however, come responsibilities, and the preservation of Mourne's exceptional beauty must always come first.

The walking routes in this guidebook mostly follow clear paths and tracks on the lower ground, and most of them continue to follow clear lines even on the higher ground. Careful attention to the route descriptions should enable you to choose a walk within your capabilities and experience. Most of the routes are circular, starting and finishing at a car park, but some are linear and you may need to organise transport to the start and finish. Many of the routes intersect, or have stretches in common with other routes, so there is ample opportunity to create longer walks using the route descriptions in this book.

The Mountains of Mourne boast two annual 'walking festivals', when walkers are encouraged to get together and share their joy of walking and their knowledge of routes with each other. These walking festivals include a thriving social side, so there will generally be an opportunity to meet in the evenings for a drink, music, singing or dancing. The current round of walking festivals takes place at

If you are lucky, you may see the rare marsh fritillary butterfly.

weekends during the summer months. The Mourne International Walking Festival occurs in late June and shifts between Newcastle and Warrenpoint (www.mournewalking.co.uk). The Wee Binnians Walking Festival occurs in the middle of September and includes not only the Mountains of Mourne, but also the neighbouring Cooley Hills and Slieve Gullion (www.weebinnians.com). Other notable events include the Mourne Mountain Marathon and the Mourne Seven Sevens, but these demand an element of speed and endurance normally beyond the reach of ordinary walkers. The Seven Sevens is a tough day's trek, visiting each of the seven peaks over 700m (2300ft) in the High Mournes, which you could attempt by devising your own route and walking at your own pace whenever it suits you best.

More experienced walkers might like to consider following the course of the Mourne Wall around the High Mournes, for which a route description is included in this book. Long distance walkers can follow a four-day stretch of the enormous 1000-kilometre (625-mile) Ulster Way, from Newry to Clough, taking in the Mourne Way and part of the Lecale Way. Full details of the Ulster Way can be studied at www.walkni.com.

Unlike most parts of Ireland, there are some routes in the lowlands around the Mournes that are signposted as public footpaths and bridleways. These are generally in low-lying countryside and are recognised by the District Councils as rights of way. The District Councils hold records of all routes in their areas that are either 'alleged' rights of way, or have become fully 'asserted' rights of way. The two main District Councils covering the Mountains of Mourne are Newry & Mourne District Council and Down District Council. Banbridge District Council covers a significant part of the countryside around Slieve Croob.

## MOURNE HERITAGE TRUST

The Mountains of Mourne, along with neighbouring Slieve Croob and the farmlands around their fringes, were designated an Area of Outstanding Natural Beauty (AONB) in 1986. The Mourne Heritage Trust, a body comprising representatives of the farming community, tourism bodies and environmental interests, manages the Mourne AONB. The mission of the Trust is 'to sustain and enhance the environment, rural regeneration, cultural heritage and visitor opportunities of the Mourne AONB and contribute to the well-being of Mourne's communities.'

The Mourne Heritage Trust has a very wide remit, and aims to involve everyone with an interest in the future development of the Mourne AONB. To this end, the Mourne Conservation Volunteers aim to offer a 'hands-on' approach to conservation, involving rangering, habitat surveys, environmental education, landscape projects and practical countryside management, enhancing the Mourne AONB. For details of projects currently being run by the volunteers, see www.activelifestyles.org.

Guided walks are arranged throughout the summer by the Mourne Heritage Trust, led by their knowledgeable rangers. These walks are a good introduction to walking in the Mournes, giving visitors a chance to ask questions and learn more about the history, heritage and wildlife of the area. Walkers who wish to learn more about the organisations mentioned above, or the summer series of guided walks, should contact Mourne Heritage Trust, Unit 3, Cornmill Quay, Annalong Marine Park, Annalong, Co Down, BT34 4QG. Telephone 028-43724059, Fax 028-43726493, email mht@mourne.co.uk, website www.mournelive.com.

## TOURIST INFORMATION

There are Tourist Information Offices around the Mountains of Mourne ready to help with booking accommodation, or advising on the opening hours of various visitor attractions. Some of them sell maps, guides and books of local interest.

Newcastle – Visitor Information Office
Newcastle Centre, 10-14 Central Promenade, Newcastle, BT33 0AA.
Telephone 028-43722222. Fax 028-43722400.
Email: newcastle.tic@downdc.gov.uk

Kilkeel – Tourist Information Office
The Nautilus Centre, Rooney Road, Kilkeel, Newry,
Co Down, BT34 4AG.
Telephone 048-41762525.
Email info@visitkilkeel.com. www.visitkilkeel.com

Warrenpoint – Tourist Information Office
Church Street, Warrenpoint, Co Down, BT34 3HN.
Telephone 028-41752256. Email info@newryandmourne.gov.uk.
Website www.visitnewryandmourne.com

Newry – Visitor Information Centre
Bagenals Castle, Castle Street, Newry, Co Down, BT34 2BY.
Telephone 048-30313170. Email: newrytic@newryandmourne.gov.uk
Website www.visitnewryandmourne.com

## THE WALKS

The walks in this guidebook offer a fairly comprehensive coverage of the
Mournes AONB, with some routes at sea level and others on the highest
peaks. There are walks in the forests and gentle countryside, as well as
walks in the wild uplands. There is also a four-day breakdown of the
70-kilometre (43-mile) part of the enormous Ulster Way, following the
Mourne Way and part of the Lecale Way. The Mourne Trail runs from
Newry to Rostrevor, Newcastle and Clough, taking walkers to the
Mournes, through the Mournes and away from the Mournes. Very fit
walkers might also like to try the classic Mourne Wall Walk, following
the Mourne Wall all the way round the High Mournes from peak to peak.

Sketch maps that allow an immediate visual comparison between any
of the walks supplement the route descriptions in this guidebook. However,
it is also important to carry an Ordnance Survey map for navigation. The
most basic scale is the 1:50,000 Discoverer Series. Most of the Mountains of
Mourne are covered on Sheet 29, but routes around Slieve Croob fall on
Sheet 20. For those who prefer to navigate with more clarity, the 1:25,000
scale Mourne Country Outdoor Pursuits Map covers most of the routes. A
similar 1:25,000 scale Slieve Croob Outdoor Pursuits Map covers routes
around Castlewellan and Slieve Croob. Ordnance Survey maps can be
bought from any good bookshop or outdoor pursuits shop, and from most
Tourist Information Offices. Harvey Maps publish a Mourne Mountains
map at a scale of 1:25,000. For some of the forest trails at Castlewellan and
Tollymore you can obtain more detailed maps, or leaflets showing the layout
of colour-coded waymarked trails. At other places you will find occasional
mapboards to supplement the information on your maps.

# ROUTE DESCRIPTIONS

Each of the route descriptions has a starting point that is identified not only by name, but also by a six-figure grid reference. All the Ordnance Survey maps recommended in this guidebook explain how to use the grid reference system. The distance for each walk is given in kilometres and miles, with the sum total of all the ascents given in metres and feet. There is also a brief indication of the nature of the terrain. You will need to satisfy yourself that the distance, ascent and terrain are within your capabilities and can be completed in whatever time you have available, in whatever weather conditions apply on the day. As weather, daylight hours and individual performances of different people vary so much, the walks are very roughly graded as easy, moderate and difficult.

There is parking available for cars at the start of all the walks, but in some instances it may only be a small space, rather than an actual carpark. Read the route descriptions to discover what sort of parking is available. A large number of the walks are served by Ulsterbus, and relevant service numbers are indicated if you wish to use them. Always carry up-to-date timetables for the bus services, which do alter according to the season. Details of services and timetables can be obtained from Ulsterbus, tel: 028-90666630. Website www.translink.co.uk/Services/Ulsterbus-Service-Page.

# SAFETY

Safety is largely a matter of common sense. If you are going walking you need to wear appropriate walking gear, which usually means warm clothes and boots, with waterproofs readily available. You will need to carry a rucksack containing food and drink for the day, a small but comprehensive first aid kit, and possibly a change of clothing. Your map and compass need to be readily to hand, and you need the necessary skills to use them effectively. It is important to remember that you should only attempt walks that are within your capabilities and for which you are properly equipped. It is also important to set out early enough that you can complete the walk before darkness sets in, especially in winter when the sun can set as early as 4.30pm. Safety is about being ready for any eventuality by being aware of what can go wrong and making sure that it doesn't have a chance to go wrong. However, accidents can happen and people can become lost, injured or caught out in darkness. If things go badly wrong and you are alone, then you are in trouble, especially as many of the walks in this book

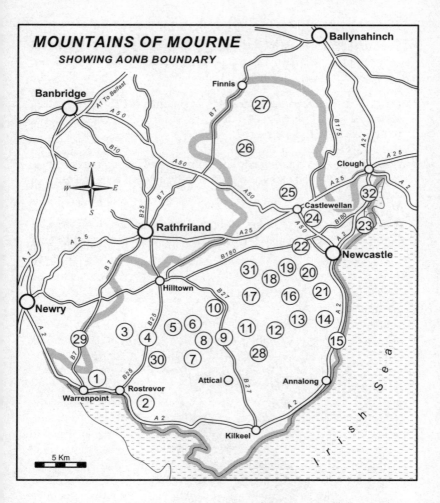

## MOUNTAINS OF MOURNE
### SHOWING AONB BOUNDARY

are in remote and unfrequented countryside, or beside the sea where tidal conditions have to be taken into account. If you have companions, then some can stay with you and others can go for help. In case of any emergency in the outdoors, dialling 999, or the European emergency number 112, alerts the Police, Ambulance, Fire, Mountain Rescue and Coastguard services. Once you have made contact, do as you are told and leave the rest to the experts. Better still, avoid getting into difficulty in the first instance. Aim to enjoy the walks in safety.

# WALK 1 - WARRENPOINT AND ROSTREVOR

**START**: The Square in the centre of Warrenpoint – 142183.
**DISTANCE**: 16 kilometres (10 miles).
**TOTAL ASCENT**: 190 metres (625 feet).
**MAP**: OSNI Discoverer Sheet 29.
**TERRAIN**: Low level farmland. The walk is mostly along roads, with a variety of tracks and paths also used. Some parts can be muddy in wet weather.
**DIFFICULTY**: Easy
**PUBLIC TRANSPORT**: Ulsterbus 39 links Warrenpoint and Rostrevor with Newry and Kilkeel. Ulsterbus 39F is a very occasional service through Burren.

The picturesque harbour at Warrenpoint.

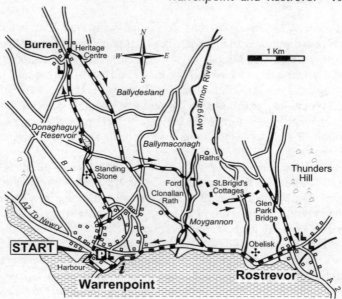

## THE WALK

Warrenpoint and Rostrevor are small but popular coastal resorts on the southern fringe of the Mountains of Mourne. Many people rush past these towns in their eagerness to reach the High Mournes, missing some intriguing corners in the quiet countryside nearby. Just outside Warrenpoint is Donaghaguy Reservoir, which lies in a delightful wooded bower, often frequented by waterfowl. The little hilltop village of Burren features an interesting heritage centre in its old National School, built in 1839. After enjoying extensive views over Carlingford Lough from high country roads, a series of little-known paths and tracks can be used to reach Rostrevor. If you object to following the main coastal road back to Warrenpoint, there are regular bus services available. Alternatively, you could head inland at one point to visit Clonallan Rath. The roads and tracks in this area are used as routes during the Mourne International Walking Festival, which is usually held at the end of June.

## THE ROUTE

The Square in Warrenpoint is situated where the harbour bites into the town centre. There is a large car park and public toilets, surrounded on three sides by shops and on the fourth side by the sea. Walk straight out of town by following the road signposted for Burren. This is the B7, which is the main road to Burren, but you leave it by turning right along Burren Road, then left, also along Burren Road. Watch carefully for road nameplates to locate these turnings, and follow the old road to the village. As you leave the suburbs of Warrenpoint there is a low grassy hill on the left, crowned with a prominent standing stone. When you reach a crossroads, turn left to enter a small car park, then keep left to follow a tarmac path around the wooded shore of Donaghaguy Reservoir.

The reservoir is quite small, rather like a pond with a reed-fringed shore. Swans, ducks, coots and herons populate it, and trees and bushes grow all the way around its margins. There are fishing stages at intervals, and a wooden bridge spans one part of the water. The path leads around the reservoir and distant views include the rugged crest of Slieve Foye. When the path runs close to a road, join the road and turn left to follow it away from the reservoir, climbing uphill alongside a putting green. Go through a crossroads and continue uphill to a junction with the B7 road near the Catholic church on the outskirts of Burren village. Turn right along the road. Just ahead is the Burren Heritage Centre, in the old Burren National School, which could be visited whenever it is open, tel: 028-41773378. There are exhibits detailing the earliest history of the area, as well as farm and household implements from the past century. The fiery workers' leader of the early twentieth century, Jim Larkin, spent his boyhood years at a cottage in Burren.

To leave Burren, turn right before the Heritage Centre, climbing up the Ballydesland Road. As you walk along the highest part of this road, views extend from Slieve Martin across Carlingford Lough, taking in Slieve Foye, Clermont Cairn, Fathom Mountain, Slieve Gullion and Camlough Mountain. Follow the Ballydesland Road downhill, ignoring other roads to the right and left, until you reach a junction at the bottom. Turn left at this junction, then left again along a narrower road. Notice how many fine beech trees there are in the surrounding countryside. Walk straight down through a crossroads, then uphill, and down to the end of Ballymaconaghy Road, reaching a junction with Moygannon Road.

Continue straight along a grassy, hedged track, which quickly turns stony and leads to a ford on the Moygannon River. You could get wet feet here when the river is high, and you should take care crossing on the slippery, smooth, mossy stones in the river. When you reach a broad, stony track, turn left and follow it uphill as it swings to the right. It leads up to a gateway. Don't go through the gate, but follow a narrower path to the left between hedgerows, bearing in mind that it may be wet and muddy later. The path winds through a wooded patch and passes a ruined cottage. Turn left to walk alongside a substantial wall, until you reach a broader farm track. Follow this track down to a road, crossing over the road to continue along another track that leads towards a house. Before reaching the house, turn right along a narrower path between hedgerows; the hedge along the right is a holly hedge. The path runs downhill and joins a road, where you turn right to walk down to the village of Rostrevor. Follow the road straight into town, passing a huddle of houses at Drumreagh Park, crossing Park Bridge, passing a Gaelic football ground and the houses at St Rita's Park. If you turn left at the end of Greenpark Road you can enter Rostrevor to avail of its shops, pubs and little restaurants. Turning right, however, leads away from the town and back towards Warrenpoint.

The return to Warrenpoint is along the main A2 coast road. There is a footway on the right-hand side, leading around a bend to pass a prominent granite obelisk. This monument was raised in 1826 in memory of Major General Robert Ross, a native of Rostrevor. Ross was very much against the American struggle for independence, and in 1814 burnt all the public buildings in Washington, including the White House. His monument was restored in 2008 and is now the centrepiece of a small park. After passing the entrance gate for Moygannon House, turn right along a narrow road that leads to a ford and footbridge. Cross the footbridge and cross Moygannon Road to follow Rath Road uphill. Just above Rathturret House, turn left and pass through a small wooden gate. A short path leads to Clonallan Rath, an impressive triple-banked circular earthwork. Being more substantial than usual, this rath was probably used by a local chieftain.

Walk back down Rath Road and turn right along Moygannon Road, then right again along the main coastal road. There is a footway on the left-hand side of the road, overlooking the stony shore and offering views across Carlingford Lough to Slieve Foye. After passing an old outdoor swimming pool, you can walk along Warrenpoint's pleasantly reconstructed promenade. This leads past palm trees and areas of greenery, passing a pier where ferries dock in the summer months, taking passengers to and from Omeath in County Louth. The promenade ends near the harbour, where a right turn leads back to The Square in the centre of town.

# WALK 2 - SLIEVE MARTIN AND KNOCKSHEE

**START**: The Square in Rostrevor – 178184.

**DISTANCE**: 17 kilometres (10½ miles).

**TOTAL ASCENT**: 450 metres (1475 feet).

**MAPS**: OSNI Discoverer Sheet 29. OSNI Mourne Country Outdoor Pursuits Map. Harvey's Mourne Mountains.

**TERRAIN**: Forested hills and open moorland slopes. Good tracks and paths are used most of the time, but some parts are untrodden.

**DIFFICULTY**: Moderate / Difficult

**PUBLIC TRANSPORT**: Ulsterbus 39 is a regular service to Rostrevor from Newry and Kilkeel.

## THE WALK

The sight of Slieve Martin towering above Carlingford Lough near Rostrevor brings to mind those famous words of Percy French, 'the Mountains of Mourne sweep down to the sea.' The village of Rostrevor and the nearby Kilbroney Park and Rostrevor Forest are quite well known and busy with regular visitors, but few climb all the way up Slieve Martin and fewer still venture beyond. There is a series of colour-coded waymarked trails in the forest, but you have to do your own route-finding out on the hills and open moorlands. This walk takes in the popular Cloghmore Boulder on the way to the summit of Slieve Martin, as well as the lonely hill of Knockshee. Long stretches of the walk are confined to Rostrevor Forest, but there are also fine views of the hills and across the Kilbroney Valley. As an alternative to starting and finishing in Rostrevor you could use the car parks in Rostrevor Forest. About 1,000 hectares (2470 acres) of forest have been planted with Douglas fir, European larch, Sitka spruce and lodgepole pine.

## THE ROUTE

Start in The Square in Rostrevor and follow Bridge Street across Rostrevor River. There is an entrance gate on the left for Kilbroney Park, and by keeping left a clear path leads up a broad expanse of grass where mature trees spread their boughs in solitary splendour. A flight of steps leads up to the Kilbroney Park Café, where there are also toilets, and even showers. Walk round the café to find a children's play area and

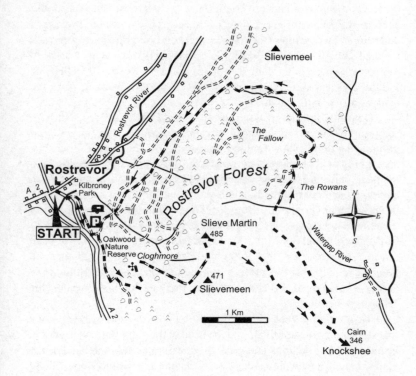

car park on the far side, as well as mapboards showing the extent of the colour-coded waymarked forest trails. It is possible to drive a car into Rostrevor Forest, park at this car park and then start the walk.

Leave the car park and turn right, downhill as if leaving Rostrevor Forest, but then turn left in front of the Forest Office. Turn left again as signposted for Rostrevor Oakwood and Fiddler's Green. The path passes an old ivy-grown quarry, and then there is a left turn at a sign indicating the Rostrevor Oakwood National Nature Reserve. Follow a gravel track uphill, bearing in mind that the oaks are the remnants of a forest which once cloaked the lower slopes all the way round the Mountains of Mourne. While it is difficult to say how much of this woodland is original, it has certainly been self-regenerating since 1730, while most other oakwoods were felled for shipbuilding timber in the eighteenth and nineteenth centuries. Other trees include ash, hazel and holly, with a ground cover of woodrush, garlicky ramsons and bluebells. Colourful jays are common in the treetops, and you should keep an eye peeled for grey squirrels, as well as for more reclusive foxes and badgers. At the top of the track, a sign points left up a narrower track for the Fiddler's Green, zig-zagging up past an open grassy clearing in the forest. There is an annual musical event in Rostrevor called the Fiddler's Green Festival, details of which can be obtained from the festival office in the town.

Continue up the grassy track from the Fiddler's Green, turning right to follow a forest track over a rise. Watch carefully for an unmarked grassy path climbing sharply to the left and follow this, zigzagging uphill between tall forest trees. It is flanked by brambles and bracken, with carpets of wood sorrel in places. The path emerges on an unplanted shoulder of the hill, and you should follow a narrow path to the prominent Cloghmore Boulder. The granite boulder weighs forty tonnes and it rests on Silurian bedrock. Legend says it was hurled across Carlingford Lough by Fionn Mac Cumhail, but geologists say it is an 'erratic', plucked from the higher mountains by an Ice Age glacier and dumped in its present location as the ice melted. There are fine views across Carlingford Lough and over the nearby hills across the Kilbroney Valley.

Turn round to face Slieve Martin and note the nearby stony track that starts climbing uphill around the head of the glen. Follow this track, keeping left at junctions and gradually turning around the head of the glen. There is a view down the clear-felled and replanted slope, taking in part of the Forest Drive and its associated car park. The track reaches a straggly fence running parallel to a ruined wall. Follow a grassy path above the forest to reach the summit of Slieve Martin, which is marked by a  trig point, or triangulation station, sitting on a cairn at 485m (1597ft). The vegetation around the summit is an unusual mix of grass, heather, woodrush, bilberry and crowberry.

Views across the sea from Slieve Martin may stretch to the distant Wicklow Mountains on a very clear day, but will more usually feature the rugged crest of Slieve Foye. Clermont Cairn gives way to Slieve Gullion, Fathom Mountain and Camlough Mountain, with the distant Sperrin Mountains in view on a clear day. The nearby hills include Slieveacarnane, Leckan More, Slieve Roe and Slieve Roosley, leading the eye round to Tievedockaragh and distant Slieve Croob. Hen Mountain, Cock Mountain and Eagle Mountain can be seen close together, with the topmost part of Slieve Muck also seen before the gentle hump of Finlieve. Slieve Donard, the North Tor and Slieve

Binnian are followed by a view towards little Knockchree and the lowland fields of the Kingdom of Mourne.

Walk away from the top of Slieve Martin towards a slender mast and concrete hut, crossing the straggly fence and ruined wall on the way. There is a crude wooden step stile over the fence if you look for it, but there is no real path. A grassy track leads away from the mast, but you should head more directly towards two shorter masts and another concrete hut in a fenced enclosure. Pass these and keep walking south-east along the broad and grassy crest. As the ground begins to fall away, the crest narrows and there is eventually a fine grassy track along its length, leading towards the rounded hump of Knockshee. There is an ancient cairn on the summit at 346m (1144ft). This is another fine viewpoint. It is still possible to see the Wicklow Mountains on a clear day, as well as Slieve Foye and Clermont Cairn, but then Slieve Martin and neighbouring heights block out much of the view further to the northwest. Beyond Finlieve to the north you can see Slieve Meelbeg and Slieve Meelmore, followed by the rugged peak of Slieve Bearnagh, with Doan also to be seen. The vista continues eastward with Slieve Commedagh, Slievelamagan, the North Tor, Slieve Donard, Slieve Binnian, Chimney Rock Mountain and Spence's Mountain. The forested hill of Knockchree and the tiny fields of the Kingdom of Mourne lead the eye round to the mouth of Carlingford Lough. It might also be possible to see the Isle of Man out to sea on a really fine day.

Retrace your steps to the gap just below the hump of Knockshee, and drift to the right to cut across the grassy slopes. There is a grassy track rising through the Watergap Valley that splits into three lines. You should aim for the lowest of these grassy, grooved tracks, then follow it gently uphill along the valley side. Some parts are firm and dry, but other parts are wet and muddy. Follow the track until you have a clear view of a forest track below you to the right. Drop downhill across the boggy, rushy slope to reach a gap at the edge of the forest, and cross a wooden step stile over the forest fence to reach the end of a gravel forest track.

Follow the track through Rostrevor Forest, staying on the most obvious track, ignoring turnings to the left and right. Eventually, the track runs alongside the forest, with the rugged, bouldery slopes of Slievemeel rising to the right. The track suddenly turns downhill to the left, with a fine view over the Kilbroney Valley. The views are lost on the descent when the track enters a stand of taller trees, followed by mixed woodlands on the lower slopes. When a tarmac road is reached at the bottom, turn left and keep left to reach a pair of barrier gates on either side of a triangular road junction. Walk straight onwards, turning right into a car park to reach the Kilbroney Park Café. On the far side of the café is the flight of steps leading to the path through Kilbroney Park that was used earlier in the day. Simply retrace your earlier steps of the day to return to Rostrevor.

The forty-tonne Cloghmore Boulder,
an erratic deposited by a receding glacier at the end of the last Ice Age.

# WALK 3 – SLIEVE ROE FROM KNOCKBARRAGH

**START**: East Coast Adventure Centre – 179222.
**DISTANCE**: 12 kilometres (7½ miles).
**TOTAL ASCENT**: 350 metres (1150 feet).
**MAPS**: OSNI Discoverer Sheet 29. OSNI Mourne Country Outdoor Pursuits Map covers most of the route. Harvey's Mourne Mountains.
**TERRAIN**: Hilly farmland. Minor roads are used for the most part, but a hill track is also used which is overgrown in places and can be muddy and wet.
**DIFFICULTY**: Moderate
**PUBLIC TRANSPORT**: Ulsterbus 39 serves nearby Rostrevor from Newry and Kilkeel.

## THE WALK

Slieve Roe is a lowly hill that is seldom spotted by walkers who fix their sights on the High Mournes. It rises between the Ghann River and Moygannon River and is surrounded by minor roads and small farms. There is a broad and clear track running along its crest, but although this is quite obvious on top of the hill, its course is less well used and more overgrown on the lower slopes. Walkers planning to walk over Slieve Roe are warned that they will need to squeeze past gorse bushes on the descent! The Ulster Way uses one of the minor roads traversing the southern side of the hill. Before approaching Slieve Roe, bear in mind that parking places are scarce and bus services run no closer than Rostrevor. It is possible to complete this walk on foot from Rostrevor, but if bringing a car into the area, please do not obstruct any road or any access to houses, farms or fields.

## THE ROUTE

The East Coast Adventure Centre is mostly used by groups and is situated in a valley full of farms watered by the Ghann River. There is no obvious car parking space on this circuit, as the roads are very narrow and access to farms and fields is crucial. Nor do buses run any closer than Rostrevor. If you do need a parking space, then ask for permission. There is a small car park attached to the Adventure Centre, though this is for the use of staff and residents. The Centre building is a prominent feature in the valley, being large and white, and so makes a good landmark for the start of this walk.

Follow the Lower Knockbarragh Road northwards towards the head of the valley, passing a junction with the Drumreagh Road. As the road rises past the last couple of farms, views of the High Mournes begin to feature away to the right. Just before the very top of the road, turn left along a broad, clear, stony track enclosed by fences. This track rises to a gate, then runs unenclosed as it passes the ruins of a few concrete huts. The track rises gently just to one side of the grassy crest of Slieve Roe, with a fence to the left. There is another short grassy track

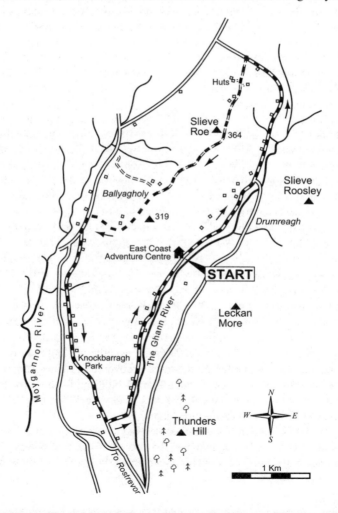

to the right which allows you to enjoy the view from the unmarked summit of the hill at 364m (1196ft).

Looking back along the crest of Slieve Roe leads the eye to Gruggandoo, then the rocky peak of Hen Mountain is followed by Cock Mountain and Rocky Mountain. Rising higher is Slieve Meelmore, Slieve Meelbeg and the jagged peak of Slieve Bearnagh. Slieve Commedagh and Slieve Donard can be seen further beyond. After the humps of Slieve Loughshannagh and Carn Mountain you can see Slieve Muck beyond Pigeon Rock Mountain. Turning eastward, the higher peaks of Slievemoughanmore, Eagle Mountain and Shanlieve come next, with Tievedockaragh closer to hand. Finlieve's gentle slopes rise in the distance, with Slieve Roosley just across the valley. Slievemeel and Slieve Martin rise beyond Leckan More. Slieve Foye's rugged crest gives way to the smoother slopes of Carnawaddy and Clermont Cairn. Fathom Mountain is lower, followed by the whaleback rise of Slieve Gullion and Camlough Mountain. The distant Sperrin Mountains may also be seen on a clear day.

The main track over Slieve Roe leads onwards and down to a gate. It continues down a slope of grass and heather with a stony, heathery embankment to the right. The course is clear and the track runs further downhill with a fence on the right, leading to a gate. Go through the gate, but when the track turns right to go down to a farm, you should walk straight onwards, stepping across a fence. A grassy strip continues across the slope, with a low wall and fence to the right. The steep grassy slope rising above is punctuated with gorse bushes. The next gateway has no gate, but a wooden pallet instead, and the continuation of the track is through a grassy, wet and muddy groove where the gorse bushes begin to press in on both sides.

Squeeze between the bushes, following a line used by cattle to reach an iron gate. After passing through this gate, watch carefully as the track swings round to the right and zigzags downhill through the fields. The track runs in a groove that can be grassy, but also has more gorse scrub in places. The lower parts are usually wet and muddy. As you pass a small concrete hut, the track is covered in rushes and often carries running water. Turn right at a larger building further downhill and go through a gate. Follow a much better track, turning left to proceed straight down to a minor road.

Turn left onto the road, then left again to follow the Upper Knockbarragh Road, which is also the course of the Ulster Way. The road rises past a small covered reservoir and descends past a few farms.

You may notice the large derelict house called Knockbarragh Park on the right. After passing a belt of oak, beech and sycamore trees, the road runs level and reaches a junction. Turn left and follow the Lower Knockbarragh Road downhill to cross the Ghann River. The road rises past Drumreagh Cottage, and later passes a number of ruined houses and cottages. The valley sides become wild and woody for a stretch, with fields giving way to rushes and bracken, then the East Coast Adventure Centre appears and the walk is at an end.

During the summer, the mountain slopes
are on fire with gorse blossom.

# WALK 4 - SLIEVE ROOSLEY FROM LEITRIM LODGE

**START**: Leitrim Lodge picnic area near Hilltown – 224256.
**DISTANCE**: 13 kilometres (8 miles).
**TOTAL ASCENT**: 450 metres (1475 feet).
**MAPS**: OSNI Discoverer Sheet 29. OSNI Mourne Country Outdoor Pursuits Map. Harvey's Mourne Mountains.
**TERRAIN**: Low hills and moorlands. Mostly on good tracks and paths, but some parts can be wet, boggy and untrodden.
**DIFFICULTY**: Moderate
**PUBLIC TRANSPORT**: Ulsterbus 33 serves nearby Hilltown and 39 serves Rostrevor, but they don't reach Leitrim Lodge or Upper Kilbroney.

## THE WALK

This walk makes use of a series of low level farm tracks, forest tracks and moorland paths. Some of these paths and tracks are well trodden, but others are so lightly trodden they are quite difficult to see on the ground. The course of the Mourne Way from Leitrim Lodge to Yellow Water is well walked. Schoolchildren from high in the Kilbroney Valley used to walk over a moorland gap on Slieve Roosley to attend school at Drumreagh. Traces of their path, known as the Scholar's Pad, are now very scanty, however. There are also tracks and paths linking farms, crossing hills and valleys, that seem to be seldom trodden these days. A combination of these old paths and tracks allows an interesting circuit to be made around the low hills and quiet valleys around Leitrim, Kilbroney and Drumreagh. It gives an insight into past farming practices as the route passes a number of derelict farms and houses.

## THE ROUTE

Leave the Leitrim Lodge picnic area by following a concrete path down to a wooden step stile beside a large iron gate. Cross a bridge over Shanky's River and follow a stony track onwards. Turn right to cross a river using a granite slab ford, and go through an iron gate in a ruined dry stone wall. You now follow a clear track across a slope of grass and bracken, punctuated by large boulders, with attractive pine trees growing singly or in clumps. The track is the course of the Mourne Way, rising gently across the slope, then passing a Mass Rock at the corner of

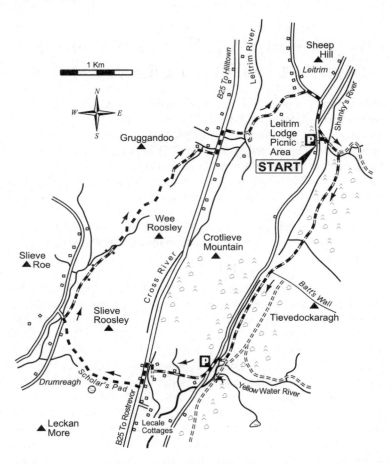

a more regimented forest plantation. The path drops slightly to cross a stream, then is quite bouldery as it rises across a rough slope of bracken. Follow the path down towards another forestry plantation, crossing a wooden ladder stile beside an iron gate. Continue along a clear forest track, passing tall trees, clear-felled and replanted areas. When you reach a junction of tracks at the Yellow Water River, turn right to pass a barrier gate and join a road, not far from the Yellow Water picnic area. It is possible to use this car park as an alternative starting point, if you are travelling up the road from Rostrevor.

Turn left along the road, then head off to the right along a forest track. This rises gently to leave the forest, passing a few houses before joining the B25 Kilbroney Road. Turn left and follow the road. There is a large house on the right, and a house numbered 131 on the left, not far from a self-catering development called the Lecale Cottages. Turn right and leave the road opposite number 131, going through a gate and following a track up to a small ruined building with a few trees growing beside it. Walk up through a gateway and look very carefully for any evidence of a trodden path up a grassy slope. This is the Scholar's Pad, which was used by children from the Kilbroney Valley attending school over at Drumreagh. The path is rather indeterminate, but you should aim to cross a broad, boggy, heathery gap between Leckan More and Slieve Roosley. On the descent, drift to the right to walk alongside a fence and ruined wall. Step over a low fence joining from the right and walk down a boggy slope of tussocky grass and bog myrtle to reach a clear stony track near a gate, road and bridge.

Turn right to follow the track. There are half a dozen more gates to go through and the track becomes covered in grass. A ruined cottage is passed, then another gate and a ruined farmhouse. Follow a small watercourse upstream from a small sheepfold, crossing it to find a grassy path on the other side. Go through an old gateway and follow the path as it squeezes past prickly gorse bushes. Step over a low fence and follow a ruined dry stone wall onwards. The path turns left when the wall turns left round a corner, then the path swings right and runs gently up a rugged moorland slope. Watch the course of this path carefully, as it is vague in places. It is a fairly clear heathery groove as it passes through a gate in a fence, then it becomes vague again as it crosses a broad gap between Wee Roosley and Trainor's Rocks. The path becomes broader and runs downhill as a deeply grooved track alongside a small stream. Follow the track down through a double gateway, and then follow a fence down to another gate beside a hut. Gorse bushes flank the track as it continues through another gate, then it runs downhill past farm buildings to reach the B25 road again.

Turn left along the road and cross two bridges over streams, then look out for a track on the right that leads down to the Leitrim River. Ford the river and turn left to follow a grassy track. The track leads away from the Leitrim River and goes through a gate where an old cottage stands in a clump of trees. One length of the track is wet and rushy, flanked by gorse bushes, leading to another gate. Beyond this gate, the gorse hedges are well clipped and the track is covered in grass as it climbs gently uphill to pass a house and join the Leitrim Road. Turn right along the road, and right again at the next road junction to return to the Leitrim Lodge picnic area.

# WALK 5 – TIEVEDOCKARAGH AND ROCKY MOUNTAIN

**START**: Leitrim Lodge picnic area near Hilltown – 224256.
**DISTANCE**: 12 kilometres (7½ miles).
**TOTAL ASCENT**: 500 metres (1640 feet).
**MAPS**: OSNI Discoverer Sheet 29. OSNI Mourne Country Outdoor Pursuits Map. Harvey's Mourne Mountains.
**TERRAIN**: Forest and rugged hills. Mostly on good forest tracks and rather indistinct hill paths. Some parts are wet and boggy.
**DIFFICULTY**: Moderate / Difficult
**PUBLIC TRANSPORT**: Ulsterbus 33 serves nearby Hilltown, but doesn't reach Leitrim Lodge.

## THE WALK

There are some interesting little hills around Leitrim and the top of the Kilbroney Valley. The Mourne Way passes through these hills, but generally stays quite low. Its course is followed through attractive stands of pines and into denser forest, then left to follow tracks high on the slopes of Tievedockaragh. After crossing Batt's Wall the route remains high to pass interesting rocky tors at Pierce's Castle and Tornamrock, followed by an ascent of the domed Rocky Mountain. The circuit is accomplished in the shadow of higher mountains, such as Eagle Mountain and Shanlieve, and these could be included by following Batt's Wall between Tievedockaragh and Pierce's Castle.

## THE ROUTE

Leave the Leitrim Lodge picnic area by following a concrete path down to a wooden step stile beside a large iron gate. Cross a bridge over Shanky's River and follow a stony track onwards. Turn right to cross a river using a granite slab ford, and go through an iron gate in a ruined dry stone wall. You now follow a clear track across a slope of grass and bracken, punctuated by large boulders, with attractive pine trees growing singly or in clumps. The track is the course of the Mourne Way, rising gently across the slope, then passing a Mass Rock at the corner of a more regimented forest plantation. The path drops slightly to cross a stream, then is quite bouldery as it rises across a rough slope of bracken.

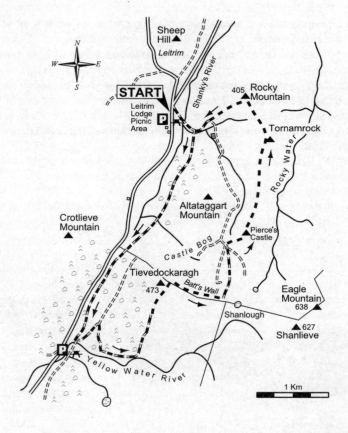

Follow the path down towards another forestry plantation, crossing a wooden ladder stile beside an iron gate. Continue along a clear forest track, passing tall trees, clear-felled and replanted areas. When you reach a junction of tracks at the Yellow Water River, turn left uphill.

You will notice a footbridge on the right, with a view of the bouldery course of the Yellow Water River, but otherwise follow the track as it drifts left, away from the river, climbing up a slope of young trees. The banks beside the track are covered with heather, bracken, bilberry and rosebay willowherb. When you reach a junction of tracks, turn right and drift back towards the course of the Yellow Water at a higher level. When another junction of tracks is reached, turn left to pass through a gateway, following the track roughly parallel to the

Yellow Water River. The track crosses a bridge over a smaller stream, but before this point you should turn left along the grassy groove of a track that runs through the forest. At first, the trees stands well away from the track and the stream, but later the track narrows to a heathery path and the trees grow closer to the stream. When the forest fence is reached, cross a wooden step stile, and then drift slightly to the left to climb the rugged slopes of Tievedockaragh. The initial boggy slopes give way to firmer heather, studded with occasional boulders. There is nothing to mark the actual summit, which is a broad and featureless area at 473m (1557ft).

A view of Rocky Mountain, from close to the Mass Rock.

Just beyond the summit of Tievedockaragh is Batt's Wall, a substantial granite construction. Cross the wall using a stone step stile, then turn right and follow it. The wall gives way to a fence across a broad gap of heathery peat hags. Another length of dry stone wall continues over another rugged heathery rise, then another stretch of fencing leads towards a broad bog. When you see another fence joining from the right, turn left and look carefully for an old bog road. This is a rather vague line at first, but it quickly becomes a clear stony and gritty track across areas of bare peat and heather. Cut off to the right to approach the prominent granite tor of Pierce's Castle, climbing to the bare rocky slab that forms its summit.

Follow a narrow trodden path to descend from Pierce's Castle, crossing more granite slabs on its shoulder, then continue down to a gap. The path leads up a grassy, bouldery slope, then runs down to another gap where heather and peat hags appear quite suddenly. There is still a path, rising from the hags on the gap to a broad summit of heather and boulders. Pass to the left of an undercut granite tor called Tornamrock on the descent to the next gap, walking on grass and heather. There is a clear path crossing the gap, allowing an exit to the left if required, otherwise simply cross it. Climb steeply uphill on grass, heather and boulders to reach a small cairn on the summit of Rocky Mountain at 405m (1326ft). Walk along a gentle shoulder of the hill, and then descend roughly south-westwards. There is a vague path avoiding rocky areas, leading down to a bend on a track at the foot of the hill. Turn right to walk down the track, crossing a granite bridge over Shanky's River. There is a wooden step stile beside a large iron gate and a concrete path leads back into the Leitrim Lodge picnic area.

# WALK 6 - HEN, COCK, PIGEON AND EAGLE MOUNTAINS

**START**: Leitrim Lodge picnic area near Hilltown – 224256.
**DISTANCE**: 16 kilometres (10 miles).
**TOTAL ASCENT**: 1,050 metres (3445 feet).
**MAPS**: OSNI Discoverer Sheet 29. OSNI Mourne Country Outdoor Pursuits Map. Harvey's Mourne Mountains.
**TERRAIN**: Mountainous. There are tracks on the lower slopes, but only vague and discontinuous paths on the higher slopes. Some sections are pathless. There are some steep and rocky slopes, as well as areas of sodden bog.
**DIFFICULTY**: Difficult
**PUBLIC TRANSPORT**: Ulsterbus 33 serves nearby Hilltown, but doesn't reach Leitrim Lodge.

## THE WALK

This walk is for the birds, taking in an area of the Mountains of Mourne where most of the peaks are named after birds. A convenient starting point is the Leitrim Lodge picnic area, although you could use a small car park beside the Rocky River Bridge. The jagged, rocky peak of Hen Mountain stands alongside the rounded Cock Mountain, with the broad-shouldered Pigeon Rock Mountain next in line. Slievemoughanmore rises steep and rugged on the way to Eagle Mountain. The descent is via the Castle Bog, which is usually very soft and wet underfoot, but there is a fine bog road leading down from the mountains. There is a surprising amount of climbing on this circuit, calling for a good level of fitness and stamina. Some parts are steep and rugged, with huge boulders of granite that can make progress slow in places.

## THE ROUTE

Start at the Leitrim Lodge picnic area, tucked away in a small pine forest on a minor road between Rostrevor and Hilltown. Leave the car park and turn right to follow the road. Turn right again at a junction signposted for Newcastle and the Spelga Dam to follow the road to the Rocky River Bridge, where there is another small car park and picnic area. Turn right and follow a fine gravel track away from a large house.

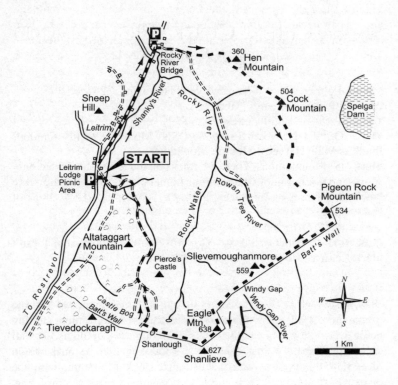

The track is flanked by gorse bushes, leading to a stout iron gate and stone step stile at the foot of Hen Mountain. Leave the track and climb to the left, up the steep, grassy slopes of Hen Mountain. There are a few boulders embedded in the ground, and a trodden path leads uphill. The clearest path is to the right of the substantial West Tor, but it is actually better to follow a less well trodden line to the left of the tor, leading a little more quickly to the rugged crest of the mountain. The Central Tor is the largest and highest outcrop on Hen Mountain. It is easy enough to walk on the granite bedrock, which is almost devoid of vegetation. The altitude is 360m (1189ft).

Follow the line of a stone gully slicing between the Central Tor and South Tor, which allows a fairly direct line down to a broad gap of grass and heather. Cross the gap, following only the scantiest of paths, then climb up the slopes of Cock Mountain. There is more heather as the ground steepens, as well as small outcrops of rock towards the top.

There are two rival summits, both bearing cairns, and the one with the largest cairn rises to 504m (1666ft). Views take in the nearby Hen Mountain, distant Slieve Croob and Butter Mountain towards the north. Turning clockwise, the gentle slopes of Slieve Meelmore and Slieve Meelbeg are followed by the rugged peak of Slieve Bearnagh. Slieve Donard rises beyond Slieve Loughshannagh. Cove Mountain gives way to Slievelamagan, Carn Mountain, the North Tor and the broad shoulders of Slieve Muck. Nearby Pigeon Rock Mountain is followed by a view through to the sea, then Slievemoughanmore gives way to Eagle Mountain and Shanlieve. There are distant views of Slieve Martin and Slieve Foye. Closer to hand are the smaller hills of Tievedockaragh, Slieve Roosley and Slieve Roe, with the Cooley Hills beyond, along with Slieve Gullion and Camlough Mountain. The distant Sperrin Mountains may be seen on the clearest days.

There are only vague paths leading off the back of Cock Mountain. A gentle heathery slope leads down to a broad and boggy gap. There are old bog roads on the gap that could be linked to provide a firmer footing, and you can study their layout on the way down to the gap, then decide if they are of any use to you. Walk up the broad, grassy slopes of Pigeon Rock Mountain to reach a corner of Batt's Wall. The summit of the mountain is broad and hummocky, rising to 534m (1755ft). Follow the wall straight onwards, passing a pool, then turn right to follow the wall downhill. There is a grassy path beside the wall, and you may notice that the wall is predominantly constructed of Silurian rock, though it gives way to granite at the bottom of the gap. Pass a ladder stile as you cross the eroded peat on the gap, then follow the wall straight uphill. Boulders and small outcrops of rock punctuate a steep slope of grass. You should notice that Batt's Wall and the outcropping rock are again made of contorted Silurian rocks. To visit the summit of Slievemoughanmore, you need to drift to the right, away from the wall. The rugged grassy top has some boggy patches and low outcrops of rock, as well as two cairns on top. The highest point is at 559m (1837ft).

As you leave Slievemoughanmore, the wall is again made of granite and becomes quite substantial on the descent. The steep slope leads down to the boggy Windy Gap where the wall is partially ruined. Although there are ladder stiles over Batt's Wall and an adjoining wall, you don't need to cross them. Continue straight uphill on the same side of Batt's Wall, on a steep slope of heather and boulders. There may be bare rock and low outcrops to cross, then the wall turns left on a gentle shoulder of Eagle Mountain. When it turns right there is a ladder stile

Rugged moorland and rocky tors on Hen Mountain.

crossing it. The summit cairn is on the other side at 638m (2084ft).

If you cross the ladder stile to visit the summit cairn, then cross back again and continue to follow the wall across a broad, gentle gap. Batt's Wall turns right on the neighbouring summit of Shanlieve. The summit cairn is actually on the other side of the wall at 627m (2056ft). The wall runs steeply downhill on a heathery, bouldery slope that becomes quite wet towards the bottom. The course of the wall ends and the line of a fence continues across the wet and spongy Castle Bog.

Follow the course of the fence, but at a distance from it, taking care to avoid the wettest parts of this bog, especially after heavy rain. Tread carefully to the far side, trying to avoid filling your boots with bog water. On the far side there is a junction of fences, and at this point you should turn right and look carefully for traces of an old track on the drier parts of the Castle Bog. This is a rather vague line at first, but it quickly becomes a clear stony and gritty track across areas of bare peat and heather. The rocky tor of Pierce's Castle rises ahead, but the track swings left away from it. Other tracks join, then the track swings right and runs down into a valley. The surface of the track is quite stony and it descends through a prominent groove, running roughly parallel to a stream. The track crosses the stream and continues down past a water intake. Follow the track downhill and cross a granite bridge to reach a wooden step stile beside a substantial iron gate. Cross the stile and follow a concrete path through the Leitrim Lodge picnic area to return to the car park where the walk started.

# WALK 7 - EAGLE MOUNTAIN AND FINLIEVE

**START**: Holy Cross Park near Attical – 260191.
**DISTANCE**: 16 kilometres (10 miles).
**TOTAL ASCENT**: 650 metres (2130 feet).
**MAPS**: OSNI Discoverer Sheet 29. OSNI Mourne Country Outdoor Pursuits Map. Harvey's Mourne Mountains
**TERRAIN**: Mountainous. There are some good tracks and paths on the lower slopes, but there is also a broad, boggy, featureless crest that can be confusing in mist or poor visibility. The route ends by following roads.
**DIFFICULTY**: Moderate / Difficult
**PUBLIC TRANSPORT**: Ulsterbus 407A serves Attical from Kilkeel. Ulsterbus 405 is a summer service to Attical from Newcastle.

## THE WALK

Eagle Mountain often fails to catch the eye in distant views. A rounded dome and a long, gentle crest are all that most people notice. On closer inspection, however, you become aware of some very steep slopes, and a fine cliff-line above the Windy Gap River. Blocky buttresses and steep slabs of granite make it a favourite haunt of rock climbers. Batt's Wall reaches its highest points while crossing Eagle Mountain and neighbouring Shanlieve. Narcissus Batt was a wealthy Belfast merchant and landowner, who had this impressive dry stone wall built in a series of straight lines across the mountains to mark his estate. While there are some good paths and tracks, and the course of Batt's Wall to aid navigation, there is also an extensive blanket bog between Shanlieve and Finlieve that needs care. The final stretch is on the road back towards Attical, passing the little-known Whitewater Brewery and lowland farms.

## THE ROUTE

This walk starts on the road known as the Sandy Brae, near the village of Attical. Parking is quite limited along the road, and you should take great care to park in a manner that will allow farm vehicles to pass, and not obstruct any gateways. If you plan to walk along the Sandy Brae, start at a junction with the Tullyframe Road near the Holy Cross Park

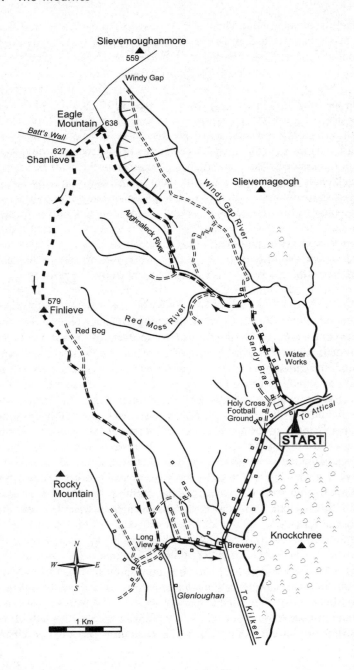

Gaelic football ground. The road rises past the Attical Water Treatment Works, then continues as a gravel track. There is an expanse of bouldery, heathery ground on the left, then the track crosses a gentle rise and descends towards a ford before the last farmhouse.

Watch carefully to spot a grassy track on the left before you reach the ford and farm buildings. This track runs gently uphill and follows the line of a fence for a while. Go through a gate in the fence and follow the track onwards. Cross the Red Moss River using a bouldery ford and note how the track runs through a deep groove in the rugged moorland slope. There are patches of bracken in the heather, and the track leads across another stream. Continue onwards and upwards to cross the Aughnaleck River too. Climb a short way above the river, and then follow the track as it bends to the left to continue uphill, though the line becomes less distinct. You will pass a point where some setts have been cut from the granite bedrock, and you can see the marks made by the 'plug and feather' tools. As the line of the track becomes vague, choose either to follow faint paths along the heathery moorland crest, or drift towards a line of cliffs overlooking the Windy Gap River. It is probably best to follow the cliff-line, which includes some dramatic views of sheer buttresses – a favourite place for rock climbers on warm days. A gentle climb eventually leads onto the heathery dome of Eagle Mountain, where a cairn stands at an altitude of 638m (2,084ft). There is a ladder stile over the nearby Batt's Wall, but you shouldn't cross it.

Views can be remarkably extensive, the vista to the north taking in the rocky little peak of Hen Mountain, Cock Mountain and distant Slieve Croob. Turning to the east, there is a peep through to the Spelga Dam and Butter Mountain between Slievemoughanmore and Pigeon Rock Mountain. The rounded slopes of Slieve Meelmore and Slieve Meelbeg are next, followed by the rugged peak of Slieve Bearnagh. Slieve Commedagh is seen beyond the smooth slopes of Slieve Muck, with Slieve Donard alongside. Further east again, Slievelamagan and Chimney Rock Mountain lead the eye to the North Tor and Slieve Binnian. Slievenaglogh pushes itself forward, then Wee Binnian gives way to the intricate field patterns of the Kingdom of Mourne and the sea. The forested hump of Knockchree comes next, followed by Finlieve, where this particular walk is heading. There is a distant view of Slieve Foye and Slieve Martin towards the south-west, then Shanlieve appears, much closer to hand. Clermont Cairn and Slieve Gullion are seen in the distance, with Leckan More, Slieve Roosley

Walkers follow the cliff edge towards Eagle Mountain.

and Slieve Roe closer to hand to the west. Rocky Mountain and Camlough Mountain may lead the eye to the distant Sperrin Mountains on a clear day.

Turn left on the summit of Eagle Mountain to follow Batt's Wall across a broad, gentle gap. The wall turns right on the neighbouring summit of Shanlieve, but you should drift away to the left to reach the summit cairn at 627m (2056ft). In mist or poor visibility, you need to be a competent navigator to follow this route onwards to Finlieve. There are no paths on the broad moorland crest, and an extensive decaying blanket bog makes it difficult to follow any straight-line bearings with accuracy. Even on a clear day, you will lose sight of the distant hump of Finlieve as you head roughly southwards towards it. This line takes you across a broad and gentle gap, where most of the bog has been washed away to leave a stony surface. Beyond the gap the crest becomes much broader and is criss-crossed by a maze of peaty channels. There are some stony areas where a firm and dry footing is available, but taking advantage of them depends on your exact course. Once you are through this expanse of bog, the ground becomes much better for walking, and the final climb onto the gentle grassy hump of Finlieve leads to a small cairn at 579m (1889ft). On a clear day you may be able to see across the sea to the south as far as the Wicklow Mountains.

Walk roughly south-eastwards to descend from Finlieve. A grassy slope leads towards the Red Bog. Turf cutting has long since ceased and the area is being reclaimed by nature, but you can still locate a handful of old bog roads leading away from the old cuttings. Follow the most obvious bog road and let it lead you further down the slope. It eventually runs much straighter and becomes quite clear on the ground. It descends across the slopes of Rocky Mountain and swings more to the right when it reaches fields further downhill. As you follow the track through a gate it becomes stonier and is enclosed by walls, fences, and plenty of gorse bushes. The track leads down to a narrow tarmac road beside a house called Long View.

Turn left along the narrow road and follow it as it bends to the right, passing fields and farmhouses. At a junction with the wider Tullyframe Road, turn left and pass the Whitewater Brewery (www.whitewaterbrewery.com). The road is remarkably straight and passes more fields, farms and houses. When it bends to the right, you will be able to see the Holy Cross Park Gaelic football ground, and the Sandy Brae road is off to the left, bringing this walk to a close.

# WALK 8 - SLIEVEMOUGHANMORE FROM ATTICAL

**START**: Holy Cross Park near Attical – 260191.
**DISTANCE**: 13 kilometres (8 miles).
**TOTAL ASCENT**: 460 metres (1510 feet).
**MAPS**: OSNI Discoverer Sheet 29. OSNI Mourne Country Outdoor Pursuits Map. Harvey's Mourne Mountains.
**TERRAIN**: Mountainous. Good tracks are used on the ascent and descent, but paths on both sides of the summit are steep, rough and boggy in places.
**DIFFICULTY**: Moderate
**PUBLIC TRANSPORT**: Ulsterbus 407A serves Attical from Kilkeel. Ulsterbus 405 is a summer service to Attical from Newcastle.

## THE WALK

Slievemoughanmore is a steep-sided mountain, tucked in between Eagle Mountain and Pigeon Rock Mountain. Batt's Wall crosses the mountain on its way from the Kilbroney Valley to link with the Mourne Wall on Slieve Muck. Slievemoughanmore is an interesting mountain from a geological perspective, as the summit is made of ancient Silurian strata perched on top of the younger granite that comprises so much of the Mountains of Mourne. This 'roof' of ancient strata has been heavily baked and deformed by the intense heat and pressure associated with the emplacement of such a large mass of granite. The walk is accomplished from the Windy Gap River on the Attical side of the mountain. Farm tracks and a couple of well graded quarry tracks are used, but the upper slopes of Slievemoughanmore are steep and rugged on all sides.

## THE ROUTE

This walk starts on the road known as the Sandy Brae, near the village of Attical. Parking is quite limited along the road, and you should take great care to park in a manner that will allow farm vehicles to pass, and not obstruct any gateways. If you plan to walk along the Sandy Brae, start at a junction with the Tullyframe Road near the Holy Cross football ground. The road rises past the Attical Water Treatment Works,

then continues as a gravel track. There is an expanse of bouldery,
heathery ground on the left, then the track crosses a gentle rise and
descends towards a ford and concrete footbridge before the last
farmhouse.

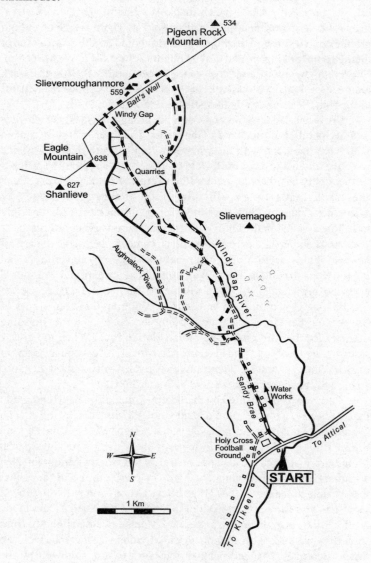

Cross the footbridge and turn immediately left, then cross a ladder stile beside a small gate and turn immediately right. Follow the boundary wall around the farmhouse and link with the track on the far side to proceed further into the valley. Watch carefully to spot a rounded boulder beside the track, which displays a line of 'plug and feather' marks where quarrymen once tried to split it. There are plenty of old granite quarries around the valley, and you should be able to see some of them just by looking around the surrounding slopes of Eagle Mountain, Slievemoughanmore and Pigeon Rock Mountain. Follow the track alongside a stout dry stone wall, but watch for another track heading off to the right, leading to a ladder stile beside a gate.

Cross the ladder stile and continue along the track, which runs roughly parallel to the Windy Gap River. The river is almost choked with huge boulders, with the water gurgling beneath them. Cross the river at a ford made of carefully laid granite slabs. The stony track leads further uphill and there is another ford to cross. Ahead, you can see that the track leads to an old quarry on the rugged slopes of Slievemoughanmore, but don't follow it any further. Instead, turn right to follow a vague path running upstream. There is plenty of tussocky grass and heather, and even if the path is vague in places, the river itself is a sure guide up to a boggy gap between Slievemoughanmore and Pigeon Rock Mountain. Batt's Wall runs across the gap, and you should cross it using a ladder stile. You will notice that the wall is composed of granite, but as you turn left and start climbing up the steep slopes of Slievemoughanmore, the outcropping bedrock and the building material for the wall change to older Silurian rock. When the grassy slope finally levels out, you need to drift to the right to reach the summit of Slievemoughanmore. There are two rival cairns a short distance apart, and the higher of these is at 559m (1,837ft).

The view is dominated by the nearby dome of Eagle Mountain to the south-east, with the more distant Cooley Hills, Slieve Gullion and Camlough Mountain beyond. Tievedockaragh, Slieve Roosley and Slieve Roe are closer to hand towards the west, while the Sperrin Mountains feature in the distance on a clear day. Rocky Mountain, Hen Mountain and Cock Mountain are nearby, while in the distance you may be able to see the Belfast Hills. Slieve Croob is more likely to be in view, and you can see Butter Mountain beyond the Spelga Dam to the north-east. Slieve Meelmore and Slieve Meelbeg in the High Mournes should be visible, with Pigeon Rock Mountain rising much closer. Slieve Bearnagh's jagged peak to the north-east is followed by the

The summit cairn on Slievemoughanmore.

domed summit of Slieve Commedagh. The bulk of Slieve Muck cuts out all but a portion of Slieve Binnian's rugged crest. The lowland Kingdom of Mourne and the forested hill of Knockchree gives way to views of the sea to the south, where Lambay Island, Howth and the Wicklow Mountains might be seen on the clearest days.

Return to Batt's Wall and follow it downhill. The wall is again made of granite and becomes quite substantial on the descent. The steep slope leads down to the boggy Windy Gap, where the wall is partially ruined. There are ladder stiles over Batt's Wall and an adjoining wall, though Batt's Wall continues straight up onto Eagle Mountain, for those who are interested in pursuing its course. Cross the ladder stile over Batt's Wall on the Windy Gap, and follow another wall away towards the Windy Gap River. There is a narrow path alongside the wall, and this links with a much clearer quarry track. Although the quarries have long ceased to produce stone, the workings are still very evident. Part of the old quarry track is actually surfaced with granite setts, though other parts are covered in grass. The rugged slopes alongside the track are covered in heather and boulders, with the towering cliffs of Eagle Mountain rising high above. When the track runs down to the bottom of the valley, you begin to retrace your steps of the earlier part of the walk. As you approach the farmhouse, remember to keep to the right and walk around the boundary wall, then turn left to cross a ladder stile beside a small gate. A right turn across the concrete footbridge leads you back onto the Sandy Brae, which you can follow back towards Holy Cross football ground, or to wherever you parked your car.

# WALK 9 – SLIEVE MUCK AND PIGEON ROCK MOUNTAIN

**START**: On the Banns Road off the B27 road near Attical – 285214.
**DISTANCE**: 19 kilometres (12 miles).
**TOTAL ASCENT**: 870 metres (2855 feet).
**MAPS**: OSNI Discoverer Sheet 29. OSNI Mourne Country Outdoor Pursuits Map. Harvey's Mourne Mountains.
**TERRAIN**: Mountainous. Road and tracks are used on the lower slopes, with some good paths on higher ground. The Mourne Wall and Batt's Wall are good guides over the mountains, but there is some pathless ground to cross.
**DIFFICULTY**: Moderate / Difficult
**PUBLIC TRANSPORT**: Ulsterbus 405 is a summer service from Newcastle, passing the junction with the Banns Road and the B27 road.

## THE WALK

This walk links the High Mournes and Low Mournes in a circuit based on the village of Attical. The Banns Road provides a clear access route into the mountains and the course of the Mourne Wall provides a route to the summit of Slieve Muck. The descent is along the line of Batt's Wall, crossing the Deer's Meadow and continuing onto the summit of Pigeon Rock Mountain. There is an interesting descent via Slievemageogh, passing some small granite quarries and taking in a little-known summit. There are attractive stands of Scots pine and larch to be seen on the descent, and the course of the Sandy Brae provides a clear route through the lower fields. The village of Attical is visited on the way back to the start, and it makes a good base for anyone wanting to stay close to the mountains.

## THE ROUTE

There are actually a number of places where you could start this walk around Attical. The car park on the Banns Road is one of them, but you could also start in the village of Attical, where The Mourne Lodge offers hostel accommodation, and Hillview House offers bed and breakfast and a chalet. Another alternative would be on the Sandy Brae, where the walk descends from the mountains, which would enable you to complete all the road walking at the start of the

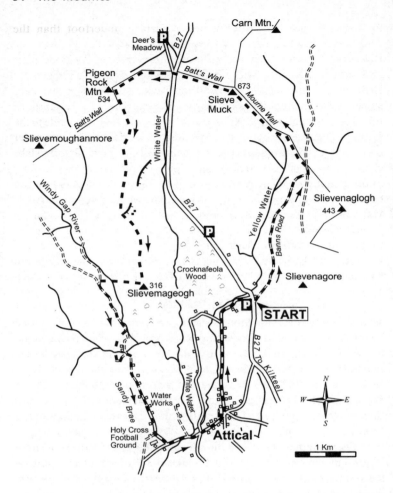

day, instead of at the end. The route description, however, assumes that you will start at the car park where the Banns Road branches away from the B27 road near Attical.

Follow the broad gravel track away from the car park. Stone walls flank it at first, though later there is a wall on the right and a fence on the left. Cross a ladder stile beside a gate and continue along the Banns Road as it heads across an open, rugged slope. The track rises over a bouldery, heathery crest and reaches a gate in the Mourne Wall. Don't cross a ladder stile beside the gate, but turn left to start following the wall across a rugged gap. There is a stony track running roughly parallel to the wall that may offer a better surface underfoot than the surrounding heather. There is a view into the Silent Valley, taking in the Ben Crom Reservoir Dam and the mountains around it. The track drifts away from the Mourne Wall and passes through a gap in another wall. Drift back towards the Mourne Wall and follow it up the steep, heathery slopes of Slieve Muck. While it may not assume the classic proportions found on other parts of the Mourne Wall, it is still a faultless guide to the summit. There are a couple of steep stretches where the wall was never built, and lengths of tangled wire fencing fill the gaps. Granite slabs cause the first gap. The second gap is on a crumbled outcrop of older Silurian mudstone. The grassy summit of Slieve Muck rises to a trig point at an altitude of 673m (2198ft) and is splendidly situated to offer views of the High and Low Mournes.

Track around the view starting from the southern shoulder of Slieve Muck to spot Eagle Mountain, Slievemoughanmore and Pigeon Rock Mountain. Turning to your right, Slieve Gullion and Camlough Mountain feature more distantly. Rocky Mountain, Cock Mountain and Butter Mountain may give way to even more distant views of the Sperrin Mountains. Lough Island Reavy Reservoir is seen on the lower ground, with Slieve Croob beyond. Looking along the course of the Mourne Wall you can see Slieve Loughshannagh, Slieve Meelbeg, Slieve Bearnagh, Slieve Commedagh and Slieve Donard. Peaks on either side of the Silent Valley include Doan, Cove Mountain, Ben Crom, Slievelamagan, the North Tor and Slieve Binnian. As the ground falls away, Wee Binnian and the forested hill of Knockchree are seen to enclose the little fields of the Kingdom of Mourne.

The Mourne Wall heads northwards along the crest of Slieve Muck, but this walk follows Batt's Wall westwards from the summit. A steep slope of grass leads downhill, with the wall as a guide all the way down to the road. The lower slopes can be wet in places, and there are a couple of rocky patches that are best avoided by stepping to the left. Cross a ladder stile at the bottom, then cross the B27 road. Continue straight across a triangular patch of rushy ground and cross a minor road to reach a ladder stile over a low wall. The Spelga Dam fills the Deer's Meadow to the right, capturing the headwaters of the mighty River Bann, which has its source on Slieve Muck.

As you cross the ladder stile, it is also useful to swing round onto the southern side of Batt's Wall, otherwise you will have to cross it later at a less convenient place. Follow Batt's Wall straight up the grassy slope, passing a few boggy patches on the way. The wall turns left on the summit of Pigeon Rock Mountain, near a small cairn at 534m (1755ft), then later turns right. Don't follow it when it turns right, but continue straight on along the broad and hummocky crest. There are low rocky outcrops and a small pool. Continue southwards to descend on a rugged, pathless slope. A broad crest of grass and heather breaks up into peat hags where there are patches of

The curlew has a distinctive curved bill, useful for probing for food amongst the moors.

crowberry. Curlews can be spotted in this lonely moorland terrain, attracted by pools of water. The broad ridge ends with a sudden steep and rocky slope, where you can see old granite quarries and ruined huts. Follow a series of grooved tracks zig-zagging downhill, aiming for a grassy track along a narrower crest. The track narrows to a path, finally reaching a dome of grass and granite at 316m (1032ft) on Slievemageogh.

Make the most of the views from this airy perch before descending westwards towards the Windy Gap River. The slope is rugged grass and heather, with some boulders, and you should aim to cross the river so that you reach a gateway in a wall beyond. There is a ladder stile beside the gate, which you cross, then turn left to follow a track down through the valley. As you approach a solitary farm, please keep well to the right and pass around a boundary wall to reach a ladder stile beside a small gate. Cross the stile, then turn right to cross a concrete footbridge above a ford. Follow the clear track known as the Sandy Brae over a gentle rise away from the farm. There are a couple of other houses along the way and a narrow tarmac road passes the Attical Water Treatment Works as it runs downhill. The Holy Cross football ground is off to the right. At the bottom of the road, turn left along another road, crossing a bridge over the White Water to reach the village of Attical. Turn left between the Roman Catholic church and the village store to follow Attical Road away from the village. It rises past a series of small farms and reaches the B27 road. Turn right here to pass the Gamekeeper's Lodge, then left to return to the car park at the start of the Banns Road.

# WALK 10 – THE SPELGA DAM CIRCUIT

**START**: At the car park on the B27 near the Spelga Dam – 268273.
**DISTANCE**: 15 kilometres (9¼ miles).
**TOTAL ASCENT**: 930 metres (3050 feet).
**MAPS**: OSNI Discoverer Sheet 29. OSNI Mourne Country Outdoor Pursuits Map. Harvey's Mourne Mountains.
**TERRAIN**: Mountainous. The hills are quite rugged, with some pathless slopes of heather, boulders and bog. There are a few good paths and tracks and the courses of Batt's Wall and the Mourne Wall are useful guides.
**DIFFICULTY**: Difficult
**PUBLIC TRANSPORT**: Ulsterbus 405 is a summer service from Newcastle, running through the Deer's Meadow close to the Spelga Dam.

## THE WALK

The Spelga Dam sits in a hollow in the hills at the Deer's Meadow, a gathering grounds for the headwaters of the mighty River Bann. Formerly, this was a summer grazing pasture, used long ago by cowherds from the lowlands, who drove their cattle into the hills and lived in small cabins until it was time to take them back to lower pastures for the winter. This was known as 'booleying', but it had long ceased by the time the Spelga Dam was constructed and the scene at the Deer's Meadow is now one of boggy desolation. The dam was constructed by the Portadown and Banbridge Joint Waterworks Board, who were investigating water supplies as early as 1946, though the actual construction of the dam was in the 1950s. The walk makes a high-level circuit around the catchment area of the reservoir, taking in a series of rugged, boggy hills. Cock Mountain, Pigeon Rock Mountain, Slieve Muck, Carn Mountain and Butter Mountain are all part of the circuit. Some parts are untrodden, while other parts have good paths and tracks. The courses of Batt's Wall and the Mourne Wall are faultless guides over the higher mountains.

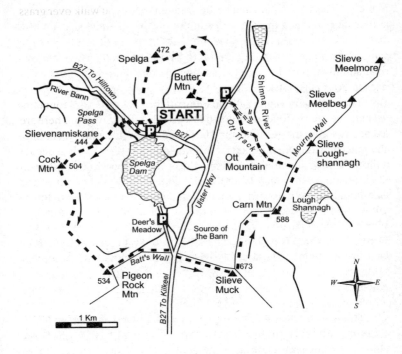

## THE ROUTE

Park beside the Spelga Dam. There are toilets across the road from the car park, as well as picnic tables. The construction of the huge concrete dam took place between 1954 and 1957. There are some statistics concerning the dam, mounted on a plaque, which may be of interest – length of dam: 345m (1132ft); height of dam: 30m (98ft); base thickness: 31m (102ft); concrete: 78,750 cubic metres (80,000 cubic yards); capacity: 1325 million litres (600 million gallons); top water level: 342m (1122ft); catchment area: 705 hectares (1740 acres); water area: 60 hectares (148 acres).

Follow the road downhill from the dam, passing Spelga House, which is available for self-catering immediately beside the huge dam. Turn left down a track, swinging sharply right at the bottom, then follow the track downstream to a footbridge. Notice how much work has been done to buttress the B27 Spelga Pass road against subsidence. Cross the footbridge and climb uphill to cross a fence near a small forestry plantation. Continue up a steep and rugged slope of heather and boulders. There is no path, but as the gradient eases you walk over grass and heather to reach the rounded summit of Slievenamiskane at 444m (1457ft). Cross a gentle gap beyond and climb uphill again, passing slabs of granite to reach the summit of Cock Mountain. There are two rival summits, both bearing cairns, and the one with the largest cairn rises to 504m (1666ft).

There are only vague paths leading off the back of Cock Mountain. A gentle heathery slope leads down to a broad and boggy gap. There are old bog roads on the gap that could be linked to provide a firmer footing, and you can study their layout on the way down to the gap, then decide if they are of any use to you. Walk up the broad, grassy slopes of Pigeon Rock Mountain to reach a corner of Batt's Wall. The summit of the mountain is broad and hummocky, rising to 534m (1755ft). Turn left to follow Batt's Wall downhill on a grassy slope that has some boggy patches towards the bottom. Cross a ladder stile over a wall, then cross a narrow road and a triangular patch of rushy ground to reach the B27 road on the Deer's Meadow. Cross over the road and cross another ladder stile over a wall, then follow Batt's Wall up the steep and grassy slopes of Slieve Muck. There are some wet patches initially, as well as a couple of rocky areas where you should keep well to the right.

There is a trig point on the summit of Slieve Muck at 673m (2198ft), splendidly situated to offer views of the High and Low Mournes. Track around the view clockwise, starting from the southern shoulder of Slieve Muck, to spot Eagle Mountain, Slievemoughanmore and Pigeon Rock Mountain. Slieve Gullion and Camlough Mountain feature more distantly. Rocky Mountain, Cock Mountain and Butter Mountain may give way to even more distant views of the Sperrin Mountains. Lough Island Reavy Reservoir is seen on the lower ground, with Slieve Croob beyond. Looking along the course of the Mourne Wall you can see Slieve Loughshannagh, Slieve Meelbeg, Slieve Bearnagh, Slieve Commedagh and Slieve Donard. Peaks on either side of the Silent Valley include Doan, Cove Mountain, Ben Crom, Slievelamagan, the North Tor and Slieve Binnian. As the ground falls away, Wee Binnian and the forested hill of Knockchree are seen to enclose the little fields of the Kingdom of Mourne.

Cross a ladder stile at a junction of walls, so that you can follow the course of the Mourne Wall roughly northwards to descend from the summit. There are outcrops of ancient Silurian mudstone along the way, and then the sudden appearance of a small cliff causes a diversion away to the right. Follow the wall across a gap, and notice how the wall changes from the contorted, banded Silurian rock to more evenly textured granite. A grassy strip beside the wall leads up onto the heathery summit of Carn Mountain at 588m (1919ft). There is a junction of walls at this point, and the Mourne Wall suddenly assumes its 'classic' proportions and is a much more substantial structure than the walls that have been followed so far. Follow the wall downhill and over a subsidiary hump, then down to a gap. Cross a stone step stile over the wall. A path leading downhill westwards from the gap becomes rather vague on a boggy, heathery slope. In clear weather you can look ahead and see the obvious stony course of the Ott Track, and once this has been joined it will lead you down to the Slievenaman Road. Cross a ladder stile beside a gate, then cross the road to reach a small car park. A granite boulder is mounted with a metal plaque giving basic information about the Ott Track and walking routes in the area.

The Spelga Dam, which holds back the headwaters of the River Bann.

A flight of granite steps rises uphill from the car park. Walk up these, then cross a ladder stile over a fence. Walk straight up a narrow path on a grassy slope, drifting left as it expires to reach the unmarked grassy summit of Butter Mountain, at around 500m (1640ft). By heading roughly south-west towards the Spelga Dam you could descend directly along a grassy path and track to end the walk, but you might like to include the neighbouring summit of Spelga to complete the circuit. Follow a faint path along the crest of Butter Mountain to reach a fence, and turn left to follow it. The fence crosses a broad and boggy gap and reaches a shoulder on Spelga where there is a little bare rock and a small pool. Turn left to leave the fence and walk past the pool, continuing along a grassy, grooved track. This is an old bog road and is wet and rushy in places. It expires before you reach the summit of Spelga at 472m (1549ft). To descend, simply head for the Spelga Dam. If you aim for the toilet block beside the road, then you will need to step over a fence at the foot of the slope. If you prefer to use a gate, then you should drift more to the left and cross a small river, then go through a gate to reach the road and car park.

# WALK 11 - THE SILENT VALLEY CIRCUIT

**START**: Silent Valley car park – 306209.

**DISTANCE**: 26 kilometres (16 miles).

**TOTAL ASCENT**: 700 metres (2295 feet).

**MAPS**: OSNI Discoverer Sheet 29. OSNI Mourne Country Outdoor Pursuits Map. Harvey's Mourne Mountains.

**TERRAIN**: Mountainous. The route starts on a reservoir road, but it also traverses some steep and rugged slopes, as well as skirting extensive bogs. There are some good tracks and paths, but in places the paths are indistinct.

**DIFFICULTY**: Difficult

**PUBLIC TRANSPORT**: Ulsterbus 405 is a summer-only service around the Mountains of Mourne, running past the Silent Valley. There is sometimes a summer shuttle bus service operating on the road to the Ben Crom Reservoir.

## THE WALK

Walkers who observe the Silent Valley and Ben Crom Reservoirs sitting serenely in line with each other may assume that the valley is long and narrow, with only the reservoirs being of particular interest. This ambitious walk attempts to show you just how extensive the valley really is. The two reservoirs naturally fill only the lowest parts, while high above there are vast gathering grounds and immense blanket bogs feeding water into the valley. If you have an interest in the construction of the reservoirs, then be sure to visit the Visitor Centre and look at the displays that chart the history of the enterprise. There are notes about the worker's settlement, known as Watertown, which was developed to house the workers. The walk wanders alongside both reservoirs, then climbs up into the mountains to follow a series of paths that allow an interesting traverse along the 500m (1640ft) contour around the slopes rising high above the western side of the valley. There is an opportunity to climb the isolated peak of Doan, which is surely one of the best viewpoints for studying the valley. The walk also incorporates a stretch of the Mourne Wall to return to the Silent Valley Reservoir.

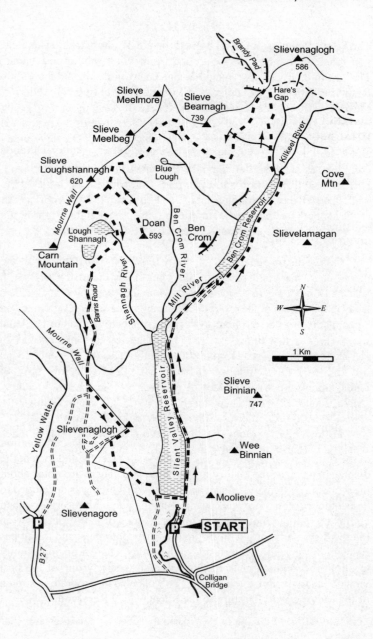

## THE ROUTE

The Silent Valley is not open around the clock, and if you bring a car you should aim to be there for around 10am, when the car park opens. The grounds around the car park and up towards the Silent Valley Reservoir dam are well landscaped with a variety of trees, shrubberies, rockeries, flower beds and lawns. There is a pool that may be frequented by mallards, and visitors are directed towards the restaurant and Visitor Centre (www.niwater.com/visitor-centre). Display boards and a short audio-visual presentation chart the history of the reservoir complex, as well as delving into the science of water catchment, purification, distribution and treatment. Don't linger too long, as the walk takes all day to complete and you should aim to have your car out of the car park by 6pm! In the summer months, check if there is a shuttle bus up to the Ben Crom Reservoir, which will save you walking the first 3 miles (5km).

Follow the road to the Silent Valley Reservoir dam. Don't cross the dam (you do that at the end of the day) but follow the road alongside it, passing through a gate beside a tower. Note the overflow funnel tucked away in this corner of the reservoir. There are some statistics mounted on a plaque that may be of interest – construction commenced in 1923 and the water was first turned on in 1933; length of embankment: 457m (1500ft); width at base: 213m (700ft); height: 27m (88ft); concrete cut off 2m (6ft) thick founded in rock 64m (211ft) below base of embankment; top water surface of reservoir: 97 hectares (240 acres); length: 3.6km (2¼ miles); width: 800m (½ mile); depth: 24m (80ft); capacity: 6600 million litres (3000 million gallons); cost: £1,380,000.

Follow the road alongside the reservoir, marvelling at how much wider it is than any of the public roads in the locality! While it is tempting always to look across the reservoir, keep a lookout on the right to spot the water emerging from the Slieve Bignian Tunnel. This is a 3.6km (2¼ mile) long tunnel drawing water from the Annalong Valley, through the base of Slieve Binnian, to augment the water in the Silent Valley Reservoir. It was cut between 1949 and 1952. There are benches alongside the road, and after passing the head of the Silent Valley Reservoir the road features a turning circle. The valley sides narrow and the rugged face of Ben Crom is seen towering above the Ben Crom Reservoir dam. Keep an eye peeled for feral goats hereabouts, with their long horns and shaggy coats. The road ends at the base of the huge concrete dam, where there is a parking space, a fountain and lush growths of rhododendron.

There are statistics pertaining to the Ben Crom Reservoir on a plaque – the foundation stone was laid in 1954 and the dam was completed in 1957; length of dam: 215m (706ft); height of dam: 38m (125ft); base thickness: 27m (90ft); concrete: 118,000 cubic metres (120,000 cubic yards); capacity: 3750 million litres (1700 million gallons); top water level: 250m (820ft); catchment area: 805 hectares (1985 acres); water area: 40 hectares (100 acres). One statistic that isn't recorded is the fact that you have to climb up 271 steps to reach the parapet of the dam! When the reservoir is filled to capacity, water cascades dramatically in white sheets from four overflow chutes.

There is a small iron gate beside the dam, with a small wooden step stile alongside, and a sign saying 'no unauthorised access beyond this point'. Oddly enough, walkers are in the habit of coming and going as they please alongside the reservoir, and there is a well-trodden path across the steep heathery slopes above the water line. The slope can be quite bouldery in places, but nowhere near as bouldery as the slope seen across the reservoir at the foot of Ben Crom. Follow the shoreline path all the way to the head of the reservoir, then ford the two inflowing rivers. You can see the Kilkeel River flowing down from a rocky gorge, while the other river slides down slabs of granite. There is a small area of short green grass here that is occasionally used as a remote campsite. After crossing both rivers, climb up a boggy slope and veer to the right to discover a stony path leading up a slope of heather and boulders. The path is rather grassier than the heather moorland alongside, so it should be easy to distinguish its line across the slope. Follow the path all the way to the Hare's Gap, where you will find a cairn built around a metal post, and the very obvious course of the Mourne Wall, complete with an iron gate.

The next part of the route needs care, and the aim is to locate a faint path contouring around the mid-slopes of Slieve Bearnagh. First, turn left on the gap to walk up granite steps roughly parallel to the course of the Mourne Wall. The steep and rugged climb leads to a more level shoulder, and at this point you should head off to the left and look carefully for the path. It contours across the heathery slope at about 480m (1575ft) where there is a slight break of slope, with steeper ground both above and below. The path is vague at first, but becomes a little clearer as it progresses across the slope. There is a stream to cross, then the line becomes less clear as it leads onto a rugged shoulder. It is almost certain that you will lose the line of the path here, so climb slightly to cross the shoulder, then look carefully while drifting to the right, on the far side of the rise, to pick up another line. The path runs roughly north-west along the lower slopes of Slieve Bearnagh, where it reaches a broad area of bog. Follow the path as it almost reaches the Mourne Wall on a rugged gap between Slieve Bearnagh and Slieve Meelmore.

Don't walk up to the gap, but swing to the left to follow the path as it contours around the slopes of Slieve Meelmore and Slieve Meelbeg at around 500m (1640ft). The path is fairly clear on the ground, being bouldery and well trodden in most parts, but it gets narrower as it approaches another gap between Slieve Meelbeg and Slieve Loughshannagh. You will see the Mourne Wall crossing this gap, and again you should turn left away from it to continue. The path runs around the rugged, heathery slopes of Slieve Loughshannagh and there is an opportunity here to include the lonely, shapely summit of Doan in the walk.

Head off to the left across a broad and boggy gap, passing peat hags to reach firmer areas of stones and grit. A path has been worn down to the granite bedrock as the slope begins to steepen towards Doan. Keep to the left side of the peak to avoid grappling too much with bare rock, and you will reach the unmarked rocky summit at 593m (1945ft). This is a splendid airy perch for studying the Silent Valley from a raven's-eye point of view. The Silent Valley Reservoir sits low in the view, followed by Slievenaglogh and the forested hill of Knockchree. Slieve Muck's broad slopes to the south-west are followed by Carn Mountain and Slieve Loughshannagh seen across Lough Shannagh. Slieve Meelbeg and Slieve Meelmore give way to the rugged peak of Slieve Bearnagh, and then Slievenaglogh and Slieve Corragh lead the eye to Slieve Commedagh and Slieve Donard. Cove Mountain is seen in front of Slieve Donard, with Slievelamagan closer to hand and rugged Ben Crom closer still. The North Tor and rugged crest of Slieve Binnian give way to the hump of Wee Binnian, bringing the view full circle to the Silent Valley Reservoir again.

Retrace your steps back across the broad and boggy gap, then turn left to contour further around the slopes of Slieve Loughshannagh. It is worth climbing slightly to reach the gap between Slieve Loughshannagh and Carn Mountain, where the Mourne Wall crosses. Turn sharply left on this gap to follow a broad and grassy path down into a valley. The path appears to lead all the way down to the shore of Lough Shannagh, but you should actually turn left to pick up a path cutting across the rugged slopes well above the lake, almost passing below the rocky summit of Doan. Drop down to Lough Shannagh's outflowing river and cross over it. You will see that the river runs in an artificial cut. There is a prominent little concrete hut nearby that is unfortunately used by some people as a repository for rubbish. Walk across an area of decayed blanket bog, featuring areas of black peat and lighter patches of grit. You will find the line of the Banns Road leading onwards, hard and stony in some places and soft and sandy in others. There are fine views of the surrounding mountains. The Banns Road leads down to a stout iron gate with a ladder stile alongside over the Mourne Wall. Cross over the wall and consider the time. The Banns Road offers an easy exit away from the mountains towards the village of Attical if you feel you cannot complete the rest of the walk.

If you are prepared for one last burst of effort, then turn left and follow the wall towards Slievenaglogh. There are boggy patches on the way to the steep slopes of rock and heather. The course of the Mourne Wall doesn't display the 'classic' proportions of the wall as observed elsewhere on this walk, but it remains a faithful guide to the heathery summit of the mountain at 445m (1450ft). The wall turns right and there is a ladder stile over it at that point. It is a good idea to cross over the wall before following it downhill. The slope is steep and is littered with angular blocks and boulders, needing great care all the way down. There is a broad and boggy hollow at the bottom, and it is best to drift to the left and follow a grassy path south-east to a prominent junction of walls. This move avoids both the bog and the circuitous course the Mourne Wall makes to get around it. Turn left to follow the wall down towards the Silent Valley Reservoir. The wall gives way to a fence, which you cross using a wooden step stile. Follow a vague path down a slope of gorse, heather and tussocky grass. A wide gravel path is joined on a bend and this leads down to a shelter beside the Silent Valley Reservoir dam. Cross over the dam, watching out for a plaque halfway across. It states that the foundation of the dam was laid at 88m (289ft) below that point on 11 December 1929. Turn right along the road at the end of the dam to return to the car park. Remember that the road out may be closed by 6pm!

# WALK 12 - SLIEVE BINNIAN FROM THE ANNALONG VALLEY

**START:** Carrick Little car park on the Head Road near Annalong – 345219.

**DISTANCE:** 18 kilometres (11 miles).

**TOTAL ASCENT:** 1,100 metres (3610 feet).

**MAPS:** OSNI Discoverer Sheet 29. OSNI Mourne Country Outdoor Pursuits Map. Harvey's Mourne Mountains.

**TERRAIN:** Mountainous. There are good tracks and paths on the lower slopes, but these become vague and discontinuous on some of the higher slopes. Careful navigation is required over these summits in poor visibility.

**DIFFICULTY:** Difficult

**PUBLIC TRANSPORT:** Ulsterbus 405 is a summer-only service around the Mountains of Mourne, running past the Carrick Little car park.

## THE WALK

Slieve Binnian's rugged crest makes this an easy mountain to identify in many distant views. Not only is the summit a monstrous bare tor of granite, but there are other tors bristling along its crest, known as the Back Castles. The Mountains of Mourne were originally known as Beanna Boirche, after a Celtic chieftain and cowherd called Boirche who ruled his little kingdom from Slieve Binnian. The Mourne Wall crosses the mountain, but does not display the 'classic' proportions seen elsewhere along its course. Instead, it is a bouldery construction with some very necessary gaps where slabby granite rock faces break its line. The route described below starts with a walk to the head of the Annalong Valley, passing beneath the summits that are climbed on the return leg. Slieve Beg, Cove Mountain and Slievelamagan are climbed before Slieve Binnian, and along the way, each successive summit rises higher than the previous one. Also, the gaps between the summits become deeper and more rugged, so that plenty of stamina is needed to complete the final ascent of Slieve Binnian itself. There is an obvious route via the Blue Lough if you prefer simply to climb Slieve Binnian without trekking across the neighbouring mountains.

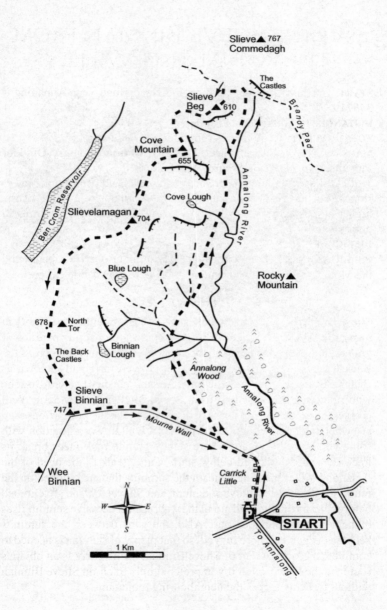

The wrinkled Back Castles on the crest of Slieve Binnian.

## THE ROUTE

The Carrick Little car park stands beside the junction of the Head Road and Oldtown Road. It can be reached conveniently by car from Annalong, but the only bus service is the occasional Mourne Rambler running in the summer months. An obvious gravel track flanked by gorse bushes rises beside the car park. The gentle ascent leads past a couple of buildings and the bouldery field walls alongside become quite substantial. Cross a stone step stile beside an iron gate. The Mourne Wall rises to the left, offering a direct line to the summit of Slieve Binnian, but on this walk it will be followed later in the day for the descent. A length of this wall was rebuilt when a couple of large fields were wrested from the lower slopes of Slieve Binnian. Some of the boulders used in the construction were unearthed by JCBs and nudged into place using machine power. Notice the large gaps in between the masonry – large enough to poke your arm through!

There is an information board beyond the gate, explaining how water is abstracted from the Annalong Valley. The water passes through a 3.6km (2¼ mile) tunnel beneath Slieve Binnian to augment the Silent Valley Reservoir. Were it not for geological problems, the Annalong Valley might have been drowned by a reservoir similar to the Silent Valley Reservoir.

Follow the rough and stony track onwards away from the wall, walking parallel to a fence, then parallel to the Annalong Wood. Although the track is rough underfoot, the slopes rising towards the mountains are even more difficult, being boggy and bouldery and covered in deep heather. The track has worn down to bare granite near the far corner of Annalong Wood. Cross a small stream just beyond the corner, then turn right at a fork in the track. Cross a larger stream where granite slabs are exposed, then follow the track over a gentle rise. Cross another small stream, and then watch carefully for a right turn, following another track that soon swings left to continue through the Annalong Valley. This track is stony and bouldery, while the slopes on either side are boggy and bouldery, covered in heather and patches of bracken. The track narrows to a path and rises gently to pass beneath a slightly overhanging rock face. This is popular with rock climbers on clear, sunny days. You will notice a cleft high in the cliff, and a heap of boulders littering the steep slopes. Cross over a stream that issues from a gully, and follow the path as it narrows even further to become a thin, peaty line. You pass beneath another towering buttress on Cove Mountain and cross another stream. The path starts to climb up a slope of heather and boulders and is braided in places. There's a view into the fearsome gully known as the Devil's Coachroad, which you will see from the top in a short while. When you reach the much clearer course of the Brandy Pad, resurfaced in places, turn left and follow it to a large cairn on a gap.

Views open up well at this point, taking in Slieve Beg, which is the next objective. Looking across the head of the Silent Valley reveals Slieve Meelbeg and the jagged peak of Slieve Bearnagh, along with Slieve Meelmore and the Hare's Gap. Slievenaglogh and Slieve Corragh towards the north lead the eye to Slieve Commedagh, which towers above the gap and features the wrinkled buttresses known as the Castles above the line of the Brandy Pad. The domed summit of Slieve Donard is followed by the Bog of Donard and a view towards Chimney Rock Mountain. This is a great place to watch the antics of ravens, or to spot peregrine falcons.

A scanty path rises roughly southwards from the gap onto the rugged, heathery slopes of Slieve Beg. Walk along the rocky edge to reach the summit, which is a little short of 610m (2000ft). Looking down from the edge you can peep into the chaotic bouldery recesses of the Devil's Coachroad, which is flanked by towering wrinkled buttresses of granite. Some walkers are prepared to climb up and down this gully, but there is a lot of loose rock and extreme care is needed to avoid sending boulders crashing down on others. Wise walkers will use a rope and treat the place cautiously, if they venture into it at all!

A vague sandy path leads down the slope away from the head of the Devil's Coachroad, descending into a gap between Slieve Beg and Cove Mountain. If you follow this path, it leads you round and across the gap, then up a steep slope of heather onto a bouldery brow. In mist it could be difficult to locate this path, in which case you would have to resort to taking compass bearings to proceed. The summit cairn on Cove Mountain sits on a granite platform at 655m (2147ft).

Leaving the broad summit area, there is little trace of a path, though one begins to form as you approach a gap to the south-west. If you use this path to cross the gap, you will find it can be traced onwards up a steep, heathery, bouldery slope that can be wet in places. The path leads past a hump on the shoulder of Slievelamagan, then climbs more directly to the summit cairn at 704m (2306ft). The path descends by weaving down a steep, bouldery, heathery slope, landing on a deeply cut, broad, wet gap. You will notice that paths intersect on this gap, offering routes left via the Blue Lough, and right down to the Ben Crom Reservoir, if any alternative routes are being considered.

Following the path straight across the gap leads ultimately to the summit of Slieve Binnian. The path is steep and stony in places, but soft and peaty in others, and there are some large boulders and low outcrops of granite that may need to be grappled with your hands. A clear path passes the huge, bare North Tor. Walkers are usually content simply to walk past it, but those who wish to climb to the summit will need to use their hands, finding the easiest line running from its eastern end. Otherwise, follow the clear path onwards, traversing the eastern side of the high crest, and rise to pass the curious arrangement of wrinkly tors known as the Back Castles. These give way to the much larger Summit Tor on Slieve Binnian. If you wish to climb all the way to the top then you will have to use your hands. The altitude is 747m (2449ft).

The view is remarkably extensive, taking in the patchwork fields of the Kingdom of Mourne and the sea, with maybe a distant glimpse of the Wicklow Mountains to the south on a clear day. The forested hill of Knockchree leads the eye round to Knockshee and the rugged crest of Slieve Foye towards the south-east. Continuing clockwise, Slieve Martin and Finlieve are followed by Eagle Mountain and Slievemoughanmore. Closer to hand, the Silent Valley Reservoir is stretched out far below, with Slievenaglogh rising from its waters. The broad-shouldered Slieve Muck is followed by a view of Carn Mountain and Lough Shannagh. Doan and Slieve Loughshannagh give way to the higher Slieve Meelbeg and Slieve Meelmore, followed by Slieve Bearnagh's rugged peak. The North Tor, Slievelamagan and Cove Mountain are all in view back along the day's walk, followed by Slieve Commedagh and Slieve Donard, Chimney Rock Mountain and Rocky Mountain to the north-east. On very clear days you may also be able to see the Isle of Man in the Irish Sea.

The Mourne Wall runs roughly eastwards down Slieve Binnian's slopes, and you will find that a path leads towards it so that you can follow it downhill. You will realise, looking back, that there is a substantial gap in the course of the wall where it abuts the Summit Tor. Follow the course of the Mourne Wall downhill, using a grassy strip close to the wall to avoid the heathery, bouldery slopes alongside. The wall leads down to the iron gate on the Carrick Little Track that was passed earlier in the day's walk. Cross the stone step stile beside the gate and simply follow the Carrick Little Track to return to the Carrick Little car park.

# WALK 13 – ANNALONG VALLEY AND ROCKY MOUNTAIN

**START**: Carrick Little car park on the Head Road near Annalong – 345219.

**DISTANCE**: 16 kilometres (10 miles).

**TOTAL ASCENT**: 560 metres (1835 feet).

**MAPS**: OSNI Discoverer Sheet 29. OSNI Mourne Country Outdoor Pursuits Map. Harvey's Mourne Mountains.

**TERRAIN**: Mountainous. The walk is mostly accomplished on good tracks and paths, but crosses slopes that can be rough, rocky or boggy underfoot.

**DIFFICULTY**: Moderate / Difficult

**PUBLIC TRANSPORT**: Ulsterbus 405 is a summer-only service around the Mountains of Mourne, running past the Carrick Little car park.

## THE WALK

A series of old quarry tracks penetrate far into the rugged Annalong Valley and walkers have long made use of them to reach the high mountains around the valley. It is now possible to walk onwards from the Carrick Little Track all the way to the head of the valley and join the course of the Brandy Pad. This long-established route, formerly a smuggling path, slices across the head of the valley and crosses the Mourne Wall. The wall is an obvious line for walkers to follow throughout the Mountains of Mourne, and on this walk it provides a series of straight-line sections leading back towards the foot of the Annalong Valley. It is while chasing the course of the wall that you have an opportunity to climb to the top of Rocky Mountain and enjoy the views around and across the valley, and far beyond its confines.

## THE ROUTE

The Carrick Little car park stands beside the junction of the Head Road and Oldtown Road. It can be reached conveniently by car from Annalong, but the only bus service is the occasional Mourne Rambler running in the summer months. An obvious gravel track flanked by gorse bushes rises beside the car park. The gentle ascent leads past a couple of buildings and the bouldery walls alongside become quite substantial.

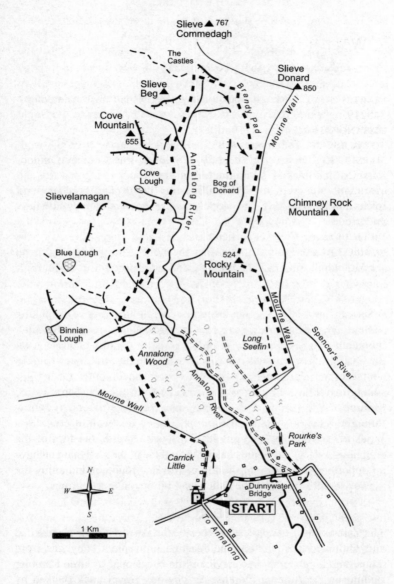

Cross a stone step stile beside an iron gate. The Mourne Wall rises to the left, and a length of this wall was rebuilt when a couple of large fields were wrested from the lower slopes of Slieve Binnian. Some of the boulders used in the construction were unearthed by JCBs and nudged into place using machine power. Notice the large gaps in between the masonry – large enough to poke your arm through!

There is an information board beyond the gate, explaining how water is abstracted from the Annalong Valley. The water passes through a 3.6km (2¼ mile) tunnel beneath Slieve Binnian to augment the Silent Valley Reservoir. Were it not for geological problems, the Annalong Valley might have been drowned by a reservoir similar to the Silent Valley Reservoir.

Follow the rough and stony track onwards away from the wall, walking parallel to a fence, then parallel to the Annalong Wood. Although the track is rough underfoot, the slopes rising towards the mountains are even more difficult, being boggy and bouldery and covered in deep heather. The track has worn down to bare granite near the far corner of Annalong Wood. Cross a small stream just beyond the corner, then turn right at a fork in the track. Cross a larger stream where granite slabs are exposed, then follow the track over a gentle rise. Cross another small stream, and then watch carefully for a right turn, following another track that soon swings left to continue through the Annalong Valley. This track is stony and bouldery, while the slopes on either side are boggy and bouldery, covered in heather and patches of bracken. The track narrows to a path and rises gently to pass beneath a slightly overhanging rock face. This is popular with rock climbers on clear, sunny days. You will notice a cleft high in the cliff, and a heap of boulders littering the steep slopes. Cross over a stream that issues from a gully, and follow the path as it narrows even further to become a thin, peaty line. You then pass beneath another towering buttress on Cove Mountain and cross another stream. The path starts to climb up a slope of heather and boulders and is braided in places. There is a view into the fearsome gully known as the Devil's Coachroad. At a higher level you reach the much clearer course of the old smuggling path known as the Brandy Pad.

Turn right to walk along the Brandy Pad, which has been resurfaced in places, following it beneath the rocky outcrops known as the Castles. These blocky buttresses are well named, featuring fanciful turrets, towers, crenellations and Cyclopean masonry. The Castles are the preserve of acrobatic ravens, while the heathery slopes below, leading into the Annalong Valley, are home to a few grouse. A couple of gullies riven through the Castles have funnelled water down onto the slopes and washed the heather away to expose the gritty soil beneath. Follow the path beneath the gap between Slieve Commedagh and

Slieve Donard, roughly contouring across the mid-slopes of Slieve Donard at around 550m (1800ft). The path leads to a stone step stile over the Mourne Wall.

Don't cross the Mourne Wall, but turn right and follow it across the Bog of Donard. The ground near the wall is nearly always wet and boggy, but becomes drier as the wall runs further southwards. Some walkers keep their feet dry by walking along the top of the wall across the bog. There is a narrow, stony path through the rugged heather beside the wall, crossing a shallow dip in the moorland. The wall turns slightly to the left, and at this point you could either follow it onwards, or make a short diversion to the summit of Rocky Mountain. There is only a vague path to follow up a slope of heather and boulders. There is a bouldery cairn, but when you reach it you will see that there is another bouldery cairn on a slightly higher outcrop further away at 524m (1718ft). Views stretch along the coast to the mouth of Carlingford Lough, then take in Slieve Binnian and its North Tor towards the south-west, with Slieve Muck and Carn Mountain beyond. Slievelamagan is closer, with the

Grouse, common game birds, roam the heathery slopes looking for seeds and insects.

rocky peak of Slieve Bearnagh beyond. Cove Mountain, Slievenaglogh, Slieve Beg and Slieve Corragh lead the eye to Slieve Commedagh and Slieve Donard, roughly northwards. Chimney Rock Mountain and Spence's Mountain complete the round.

Walk roughly south-east from the summit of Rocky Mountain to return to the Mourne Wall. There are a series of small quarries on the slopes of Rocky Mountain, with vague zig-zag paths on the rocky, heathery slopes. Try and link these paths to reach a partially walled gap in the Mourne Wall. Turn right to follow the wall along a heathery shoulder to Long Seefin. There is a stony, gritty path alongside. Alternatively, follow a path which drifts away from the wall southwards down the slope, though it does get rather bouldery later. The Mourne Wall on Long Seefin reaches a curious little stone tower at a corner. Follow the wall straight down a rugged slope, alongside a forest, to reach an iron gate leading onto a walled track.

Turn left to follow the track through a small part of the forest, going through another gate to leave the forest. Keep straight on along the track, with the forest to the left and gorse bushes to the right. The track, known as the Dunnywater Track, is grass and bare granite, but later it is surfaced with gravel as it passes farms and houses. When you reach the road below, turn right and follow it. There is a prominent water works gateway, featuring four pinnacled towers. Continue along the road, crossing the Dunnywater Bridge, climbing back up to the Carrick Little car park to complete the circuit.

# WALK 14 - CHIMNEY ROCK MOUNTAIN

**START**: Bloody Bridge on the A2 coast road south of Newcastle – 388271.

**DISTANCE**: 12 kilometres (7¾ miles).

**TOTAL ASCENT**: 680 metres (2230 feet).

**MAPS**: OSNI Discoverer Sheet 29. OSNI Mourne Country Outdoor Pursuits Map. Harvey's Mourne Mountains.

**TERRAIN**: Mountainous. There are some good paths, but also rugged, pathless slopes needing care. A rugged coastal path is followed at the end where very high tides could be a problem. Some rocks on the coast are quite slippery.

**DIFFICULTY**: Moderate / Difficult

**PUBLIC TRANSPORT**: Ulsterbus 37 is a regular service linking Bloody Bridge with Newcastle and Kilkeel. Ulsterbus 405 also passes in the summer.

## THE WALK

Most walkers who walk in the Mournes will pass close to Chimney Rock Mountain at some point. There are well-walked paths on the slopes of Slieve Donard, and plenty of people trek along the Brandy Pad, but few make their way to the summit of Chimney Rock Mountain. The Mourne Wall crosses its shoulder and Bloody Bridge, where the mountain dips its feet in the sea, is a popular place for visitors, but hardly anyone thinks to climb to the top. This walk is exclusively devoted to Chimney Rock Mountain, accessing its slopes from Bloody Bridge, following the Mourne Wall onto its shoulder, then making a summit bid. The descent to the sea is particularly rugged and bears hardly any trace of a path. The circuit is completed with a walk along the rugged Mourne Coastal Path to return to Bloody Bridge.

## THE ROUTE

Bloody Bridge is on the busy coastal road between Newcastle and Kilkeel. There is a car park and toilet block beside the bridge, and the walk starts on the opposite side of the road, where a National Trust plaque reads 'Bloody Bridge'. Go through a small gate and a wooden squeeze stile. The old Bloody Bridge lies off to the left, a single stone arch over the

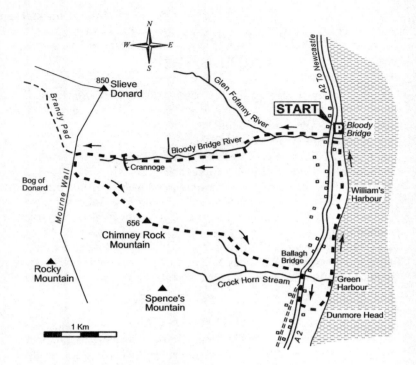

Bloody Bridge River. It was the scene of a massacre in 1641, when the Magennises ambushed a band of Presbyterian prisoners being led between jails in Newry and Newcastle. The path to follow runs straight upstream between banks of gorse, becoming rather rough and bouldery by the time a footbridge spans the inflowing Glen Fofanny River.

Continue following the path upstream beside the Bloody Bridge River, crossing a wooden step stile at a point where two pipelines cross the river. These carry water from the Silent Valley to Belfast. The path runs further upstream until it passes a part of the river where the water slides down tilted slabs of granite. Cross over the river and follow a fenced track uphill. Turn right at a junction with another track, which twists and turns, then follow it straight uphill parallel to the Bloody Bridge River. The surface is broad and clear, but also rough and stony. Watch carefully for another track that cuts off to the right and cross back over the river to continue upstream. Do not walk all the way up the track into an old quarry. (If the Bloody Bridge River is in spate and you cannot ford it, you can stay on the northern bank the whole time.) The track is grassy in some places, but is a stony groove in others. There is a heap of quarry spoil on the other side of the river, and at this point the track makes a curve away from the river. Further upstream, the path is bouldery and braided, cutting through peat and heather as it climbs. A single broad path finally reaches the Mourne Wall on the edge of the Bog of Donard. There is a view from the boggy gap, turning clockwise, of Chimney Rock Mountain, Rocky Mountain, Slieve Binnian and its North Tor, followed by Slievelamagan, Cove Mountain, Slieve Beg, Slieve Commedagh and lofty Slieve Donard.

Don't cross the Mourne Wall, but turn left and follow it across the squelchy Bog of Donard. The wall rises gently onto a heathery crest. Turn left away from the wall, following a narrow path through the heather, rising past rounded boulders to reach rocky outcrops of granite along the crest of Chimney Rock Mountain. There is a cairn overlooking a bouldery brow at 656m (2152ft). Views take in the neighbouring shoulder of Spence's Mountain to the south, then stretch across the patchwork fields of the Kingdom of Mourne to Carlingford Lough and Slieve Foye. Slieve Binnian and its North Tor are followed

The old Bloody Bridge, scene of a massacre of Presbyterian prisoners in 1641.

by a peep at Slieve Muck through a deep gap before Slievelamagan raises its rugged slopes. Through the next gap you can see the rounded Slieve Meelbeg and the rocky peak of Slieve Bearnagh, with Cove Mountain closer to hand. Slieve Beg, Slievenaglogh and Slieve Corragh lead the eye to Slieve Commedagh and Slieve Donard, roughly to the north. Dundrum Inner Bay, Dundrum Outer Bay and the slender St John's Point complete the panorama. The Isle of Man may be seen in the Irish Sea on a clear day.

Clear weather is an advantage on the descent, as the eastern slopes of Chimney Rock Mountain are steep, rugged and pathless. The first part of the descent is on a slope of heather and large boulders, which needs care. Next, the aim is to walk roughly parallel to the Crock Horn Stream, on its northern side, to reach the main coastal road near Ballagh Bridge. Keep well away from the course of the river to avoid areas of bracken, and you might make use of a few faint sheep paths down the heathery slope. Towards the foot of the Crock Horn Stream, a water pipeline spans the river, carrying water from the Silent Valley to Belfast. Step over a low fence above the river, and then walk down a slope of short gorse scrub. Use faintly trodden paths to reach a small gate, then continue down another slope of gorse scrub. A larger gate leads onto the Glasdrumman Road near Ballagh Bridge.

Turn right along the busy road, and then look out on the left for a grassy track bounded by walls and fences. Walk down this track and continue along a narrower grassy path flanked by gorse bushes. The path swings left and runs down a slope of reeds to reach a rocky shore. Turn left to walk along the shore, taking care, as the rock is often very smooth and can be slippery. Continue along a bouldery storm beach, which gives way to smaller cobbles and shingle. At Green Harbour you ford the Crock Horn Stream and there is an old rusting boat winch alongside. Further along, look out for traces of a path above the shingle storm beach, and take care to follow a path uphill once you find large slabs of rock above the shore. The Mourne Coastal Path rises above the rocky shore around William's Harbour, where it is said that Williamite troops were landed in 1689. Keep to the right at a junction of paths. Go through a small gate, and later cross a wooden step stile. A path climbing steeply uphill on the left leads to the ruins of St Mary's Church, where only a single arch now remains. Staying on the coastal path, however, cross another wooden step stile and follow it gently uphill to cross the Bloody Bridge River. A gate leads onto the busy main road, and the car park where the walk started is just beyond.

# WALK 15 - THE MOURNE COASTAL PATH

**START**: Bloody Bridge on the A2 coast road south of Newcastle – 388271.

**FINISH**: Annalong Cornmill by the harbour in Annalong – 377198.

**DISTANCE**: 8 kilometres (5 miles).

**TOTAL ASCENT**: 15 metres (50 feet).

**MAPS**: OSNI Discoverer Sheet 29. OSNI Mourne Country Outdoor Pursuits Map. Harvey's Mourne Mountains.

**TERRAIN**: Coastal walking. Includes some good coastal paths, but also rugged storm beaches, boulders and slippery ridges of rock. Very high tides could be a problem in places, so consult local tide tables before starting.

**DIFFICULTY**: Easy / Moderate

**PUBLIC TRANSPORT**: Ulsterbus 37 is a regular service linking Bloody Bridge and Annalong with Newcastle and Kilkeel. Ulsterbus 405 also passes Bloody Bridge in the summer.

## THE WALK

The Mourne Coastal Path is rather disjointed, comprising some good coastal paths and some walking along a remarkably rugged shore. There is a shingle storm beach that can be quite bouldery in places. Some parts of the coast feature ridges of bare rock, polished by the sea to reveal attractive colourful bands and veins in the rock. Look more carefully at this Silurian bedrock and you can discern darker and much younger dykes of intrusive igneous rock. The land immediately above the shore is steep and rugged at first, but later gives way to level fields. Depending on the tides and the season, a variety of gulls, waders and divers can be spotted, as well as seals basking on isolated rocks. The Annalong Cornmill is an interesting restored watermill at the end of the walk, though you should check opening times in advance if you wish to make a visit (tel: 028-43768736). Also bear in mind that this walk is linear and you should be aware of the bus services linking the start and finishing points.

## THE ROUTE

There is a car park and toilet block at Bloody Bridge, on the main A2 coastal road south of Newcastle. Start the walk on the south side of the

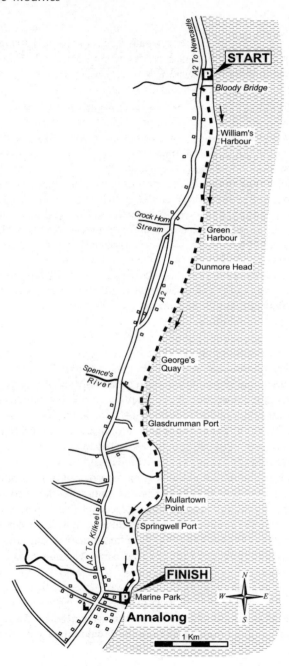

car park, where there is a small gate and a National Trust sign for the
Mourne Coastal Path. Follow the path across the Bloody Bridge River.
The original Bloody Bridge is actually upstream some distance from
the current road bridge. It was the scene of a massacre in 1641, when the
Magennises ambushed a band of Presbyterian prisoners being led
between jails in Newry and Newcastle. The path runs gently downhill to
reach a wooden step stile. There is a path climbing uphill to the right,
signposted for St Mary's Church. This provides an interesting
diversion, though all that remains of the church is a single stone arch.
The coastal path, however, crosses another wooden step stile and a
wooden footbridge, then later goes through a small gate. The path leads
down to the shore beside some large tilted slabs of rock, passing
William's Harbour, said to be where Williamite troops landed in 1689.

There is a scanty path above the shingle storm beach, but later you
need to walk on shingle and boulders. At Green Harbour, ford the Crock
Horn Stream and pass an old rusting boat winch. The shingle beach
gives way to larger boulders and ridges of attractively banded rock.
Darker dykes of igneous rock can be distinguished here, cutting
through the bedrock. There is a path rising inland up a slope of reeds, if
you decide that the going is too rough. To continue onwards, take care
as you cross the slippery bedrock and pass little rock pools. Isolated
rocks out to sea provide basking places for seals and perches for
cormorants. After negotiating the rugged shore at Dunmore Head, a
shingle beach is followed by a pleasant stretch of grassy path and a track
leads to a gate at George's Quay. Don't go through the gate, which in
any case bears a sign forbidding access.

After fording Spence's River, continue past a couple of houses and
follow the shingle beach around Glasdrumman Port. The little bay was
the scene of a fracas towards the end of the eighteenth century, when the
local exciseman Alexander Chesney came under gunfire while trying to
intercept smugglers. A narrow grassy path can be traced around
Mullartown Point, but there are some places where erosion has taken a
bite out of the land, taking the line of the path with it. Notice how the
beach cobbles have been used to make dry stone walls around the low
fields on Mullartown Point. As you walk around Springwell Port with a
view towards the village of Annalong, parts of the path have been
buttressed against erosion by using wire cages filled with beach
cobbles. As the path draws closer to Annalong, a broader track leads
along the coast, almost to the harbour. You reach a large red fishing boat
called the Castle Bay, which is permanently marooned on dry land, part

of Annalong's marine park. You could inspect the Annalong Cornmill, a working watermill beside the harbour. Its wheel turned from 1820 until the 1960s, and after a period lying idle it was restored to working order again in 1985. Annalong also has luxury hostel and self catering, a small range of bars and restaurants, as well as toilets and car parking. Ulsterbus 37 links Annalong with Bloody Bridge, if you need to return for a parked car.

This stone arch is all that remains of St Mary's church, near to Bloody Bridge.

# WALK 16 – THE BRANDY PAD FROM EAST TO WEST

**START**: Bloody Bridge on the A2 coast road south of Newcastle – 388271.

**FINISH**: The Cecil Newman car park at Trassey near Bryansford – 311314.

**DISTANCE**: 12 kilometres (7½ miles).

**TOTAL ASCENT**: 590 metres (1935 feet).

**MAPS**: OSNI Discoverer Sheet 29. OSNI Mourne Country Outdoor Pursuits Map. Harvey's Mourne Mountains.

**TERRAIN**: Mountainous. Good tracks and paths for the most part, but some stretches are rough and bouldery and can be wet underfoot.

**DIFFICULTY**: Moderate

**PUBLIC TRANSPORT**: Ulsterbus 37 links Bloody Bridge with Newcastle and Kilkeel. Ulsterbus 34 and 34B are infrequent services running close to Trassey. Ulsterbus 405 also passes close to Trassey in the summer.

## THE WALK

The Brandy Pad is an old smuggling path that has become one of the classic walking routes through the Mountains of Mourne. In the eighteenth century the rugged coast south of Newcastle was a favourite place for landing contraband goods shipped from the Isle of Man. Brandy was a favourite, but other goods included tea, coffee, tobacco, soap, wine and indeed anything that attracted a heavy enough rate of duty to be worth the trip over the mountains. Pack ponies were loaded and funnelled up the Bloody Bridge River to the Bog of Donard. After contouring around the head of the Annalong Valley and the Silent Valley, the ponies reached the Hare's Gap and exited from the mountains by way of Trassey. Now well inland, away from the eyes of the excisemen, goods were conveyed to Hilltown for further distribution. No doubt the Brandy Pad was very lightly trodden in its early days, but it became a popular walking route and is now a very obvious line on the ground. Some sections of the path are badly eroded and parts have been reconstructed. As this is a linear route through the mountains, you need to be sure you have transport at the finishing point, or be absolutely sure of the bus times.

## THE ROUTE

Bloody Bridge is on the busy coastal road between Newcastle and Kilkeel. There is a car park and toilet block beside the bridge, and the walk starts on the opposite side of the road, where a National Trust plaque reads 'Bloody Bridge'. Go through a small gate and a wooden squeeze stile. The old Bloody Bridge lies off to the left, a single stone arch over the Bloody Bridge River. It was the scene of a massacre in 1641, when the Magennises ambushed a band of Presbyterian prisoners being led between jails in Newry and Newcastle. The path to follow runs straight upstream between banks of gorse, becoming rather rough and bouldery by the time a footbridge spans the inflowing Glen Fofanny River.

Continue following the path upstream beside the Bloody Bridge River, crossing a wooden step stile at a point where two pipelines cross the river. These carry water from the Silent Valley to Belfast. The path runs further upstream until it passes a part of the river where the water slides down tilted slabs of granite. Cross over the river and follow a fenced track uphill. Turn right at a junction with another track, which twists and turns, then follow it straight uphill parallel to the Bloody Bridge River. The surface is broad and clear, but also rough and stony. Watch carefully for another track that cuts off to the right and cross back over the river to continue upstream. Do not walk all the way up the track into an old quarry. (If the Bloody Bridge River is in spate and you cannot ford it, you can stay on the northern bank the whole time.) The track

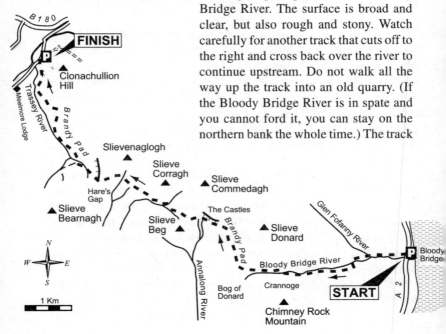

is grassy in some places, but is a stony groove in others. There is a heap of quarry spoil on the other side of the river, and at this point the track makes a curve away from the river. Further upstream, the path is bouldery and braided, cutting through peat and heather as it climbs. A single broad path finally reaches the Mourne Wall on the edge of the Bog of Donard. There is a view from the boggy gap of Chimney Rock Mountain to the south and then, turning clockwise, Rocky Mountain, Slieve Binnian and its North Tor, followed by Slievelamagan, Cove Mountain, Slieve Beg, Slieve Commedagh and lofty Slieve Donard.

Cross a stone step stile over the Mourne Wall and follow the path away from the wall. The Brandy Pad drifts to the right, roughly contouring across the mid-slopes of Slieve Donard at around 550m (1800 feet). Keep to the left at a junction of paths to pass beneath the prominent gap between Slieve Donard and Slieve Commedagh, then walk beneath the wrinkled rocky outcrop known as the Castles. These blocky buttresses are well named, featuring fanciful turrets, towers, crenellations and Cyclopean masonry. The Castles are the preserve of acrobatic ravens, while the heathery slopes below, leading into the Annalong Valley, are home to a few grouse. A couple of gullies riven through the Castles have funnelled water down onto the slopes and washed the heather away to expose the gritty soil beneath. Some parts of the path have been resurfaced, leading up to a large cairn on the gap between Slieve Commedagh and Slieve Beg. Views at this point take in Slieve Beg, then stretch across the head of the Silent Valley to Slieve Meelbeg to the west, the jagged peak of Slieve Bearnagh and Slieve Meelmore. Hare's Gap comes next, where this walk is heading, then Slievenaglogh and Slieve Corragh lead the eye to Slieve Commedagh, which towers above the buttresses of the Castles. The domed summit of Slieve Donard is followed by the Bog of Donard and Chimney Rock Mountain.

Follow the rugged path downhill from the gap, passing an eroded cleft in the granite where there is a curious upstanding pillar of rock. There is a view down to the Ben Crom Reservoir, which is overlooked by the rugged peak of Ben Crom. The Brandy Pad leads gently down to the Hare's Gap, where there is a cairn built around a metal post. The Mourne Wall crosses the gap, while the steep and rocky slopes of Slieve Bearnagh tower overhead.

Go through a gate in the Mourne Wall and walk straight downhill. The slope at the head of the valley is bouldery and usually wet. Take care not to turn an ankle on the way down. The path is vague

The Brandy Pad, looking towards the Ben Crom Reservoir.

but gets better as it levels out, fording a river and joining a track. Ford the river again and simply follow the Trassey Track down through the rugged, heathery valley. The track is roughly parallel to the Trassey River, but drifts away from it in a broad loop to reach a gate beside a sheepfold at the corner of Clonachullion Wood. Follow the track onwards, with the forest to the right and gorse bushes to the left. Go through another gate and enter part of Clonachullion Wood. At a final gate, cross a step stile beside the gate to reach a minor road. Turn right and walk a short way down the road. Just to the right is the Cecil Newman car park and picnic site. Either turn right and follow the road across the Shimna River to link with a limited bus service at the top of the Trassey Road, or turn left to reach Meelmore Lodge, which offers bed and breakfast, campsite and a café. Telephone 028-43726657, website meelmorelodge.co.uk.

# WALK 17 - SLIEVE MEELBEG AND SLIEVE MEELMORE

**START:** The Ott Track car park on the Slievenaman Road – 281279.

**DISTANCE:** 13 kilometres (8 miles).

**TOTAL ASCENT:** 725 metres (2380 feet).

**MAPS:** OSNI Discoverer Sheet 29. OSNI Mourne Country Outdoor Pursuits Map. Harvey's Mourne Mountains.

**TERRAIN:** Mountainous. Roads and clear tracks are used on the lower slopes, but some paths can be steep and rocky, or boggy in places.

**DIFFICULTY:** Moderate / Difficult

**PUBLIC TRANSPORT:** Ulsterbus 405 is a summer service from Newcastle, running along the Slievenaman Road and passing the Ott Track.

## THE WALK

Slieve Meelbeg and Slieve Meelmore are inseparable twins bound together by the Mourne Wall. In views from the north they appear similar in form, but from other directions Slieve Meelbeg tends always to be dome-shaped, while Slieve Meelmore has a longer summit crest. Slieve Meelbeg translates as the 'Little Bald Mountain' while Slieve Meelmore translates as the 'Big Bald Mountain'. This is strange, as Slieve Meelbeg is actually a little taller than Slieve Meelmore, but again, when viewed from the north, the opposite seems to be true. It is an illusion, caused because Slieve Meelmore rises in front of Slieve Meelbeg. You can climb both mountains via the Ott Track, along with Slieve Loughshannagh, following the Mourne Wall to link the summits. The descent to Trassey links with the Mourne Way, which leads back to the start via Fofanny Dam. This walk could also start and finish at Meelmore Lodge, which offers bed and breakfast, campsite and a café. Telephone 028-43726657, website meelmorelodge.co.uk.

## THE ROUTE

The Ott Track starts on the Slievenaman Road between Trassey and the Spelga Dam. There is a sign saying 'Welcome to Down District' and a small car park just beside the road. A granite boulder is mounted with a metal plaque giving basic information about the Ott Track and walking routes in the area. The Ott Track is across the road from the car park, where a ladder stile stands near a gate. Cross the stile and follow the

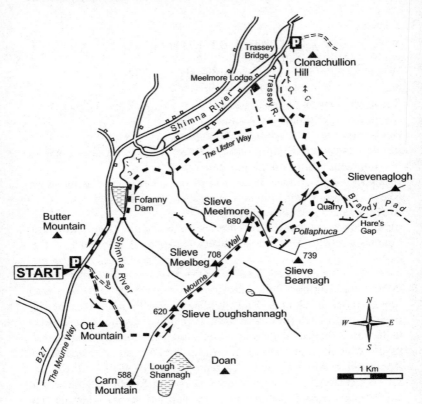

track away from the road, turning right at a junction, as marked by a yellow arrow on a rock. The track is clear and stony as it rises across a rugged, grassy slope. Follow it until it expires, then continue along a vague, boggy path up to a gap between Carn Mountain and Slieve Loughshannagh. The Mourne Wall crosses the gap, and the view beyond it reveals Slievelamagan, Doan, the North Tor, Slieve Binnian, Wee Binnian and the sea.

Cross the Mourne Wall using a stone step stile and turn left uphill. There is a strip of short grass beside the wall, with heather and bilberry stretching away from it. The wall leads to the summit of Slieve Loughshannagh at 620m (2030ft), where there are low rounded boulders of granite and a small cairn. Views are developing very well, but save them for study from Slieve Meelbeg. Walk steeply down to the next gap on the grassy strip close to the wall, with more rugged grass and heather slopes further away. The wall leads steeply uphill, still with a grassy strip close by, and heather and small boulders further away. The gradient eases towards the top, where the Mourne Wall turns right. There is a cairn on the other side of the wall marking the summit of Slieve Meelbeg at 708m (2310ft).

Looking ahead, you can see a tower on Slieve Meelmore, and there is a peep through a gap to Dundrum Bay. Slieve Commedagh's smooth slopes are seen rising beyond Slieve Bearnagh's rocky tors. Slieve Donard, Cove Mountain, Chimney Rock Mountain and Slievelamagan lead the

The heron, a large wading bird, with its long legs and bill and S-shaped neck.

eye round to a pronounced gap, where the sea can be spotted. The North Tor and rocky crest of Slieve Binnian give way to Wee Binnian, the Silent Valley, Doan and Slievenaglogh. Knockchree is seen rising above the low fields of the Kingdom of Mourne, then Lough Shannagh and the mouth of Carlingford Lough are seen before the bulk of Slieve Muck. After Slieve Loughshannagh, there is a view of the distant Slieve Foye. Eagle Mountain is closer, and then the far distance includes the Cooley Hills and Slieve Gullion. The Spelga Dam is closer, surrounded by Cock Mountain, Hen Mountain and Butter Mountain. Lough Island Reavy Reservoir is to the north, with Slieve Croob also in view.

Follow the wall down a steep slope of short grass embedded with small boulders. Pass a ladder stile on the gap, and then let the wall lead you up a stony slope onto Slieve Meelmore. The wall crosses a heathery shoulder, then climbs up another stony slope. Notice how the Mourne Wall slices through the course of an older stone wall. Follow the wall along the crest, crossing the highest part of the mountain. There is a stout granite lookout tower, built in 1921, tucked into a sharp corner in the wall at 680m (2237ft). Some maps wrongly credit this point with a much greater height.

A steep and stony slope, littered with angular boulders and some rocksteps, leads down to a deeply cut gap. There is a ladder stile over the Mourne Wall, which you should cross, unless you wish to climb Slieve Bearnagh from this point. After crossing the stile, a rough path leads down into a rugged valley called Pollaphuca. Follow the path across the slopes on the right-hand side of the valley. Avoid a quarry on the lower slopes of Slieve Bearnagh, keeping left to follow the path further downhill. When a broad track is reached at the bottom of the valley, turn left to ford the Trassey River. Follow the Trassey Track down through the valley to reach a gate at the corner of Clonachullion Wood.

Don't go through the gate, but turn left to cross the Trassey River. There is a vague path running roughly parallel to a wall across the foot of Slieve Meelmore. Following this wall leads you gently uphill, then a ladder stile and steps lead down to a stream.Climb up from the stream to follow the Mourne Way, which follows a path bearing concrete posts, contouring around the lower slopes of Slieve Meelmore. The path is actually on top of a pipeline, which is occasionally visible above the ground. It leads round to the Fofanny Dam. Cross a ladder stile and cross a footbridge, but turn left and don't cross the dam. Follow an embankment beside the reservoir, which is fringed with gorse bushes. Look out for herons, which fish in the reservoir. As you walk past the head of the reservoir, there is a view back to the dam with Slieve Croob rising beyond. The path leads through a corner of a forest, where the ground might be wet and muddy, then you walk up a grassy, rushy slope. Cross a ladder stile near a gate to join the Slievenaman Road. There is a Mourne Way signpost beside the road, and by turning left to follow the road uphill you quickly return to the car park near the Ott Track.

The granite lookout tower on the top of Slieve Meelmore.

# WALK 18 - SLIEVE BEARNAGH FROM TRASSEY

**START**: The Cecil Newman car park at Trassey near Bryansford – 311314.

**DISTANCE**: 10 kilometres (6 miles).

**TOTAL ASCENT**: 600 metres (1970 feet).

**MAPS**: OSNI Discoverer Sheet 29. OSNI Mourne Country Outdoor Pursuits Map. Harvey's Mourne Mountains.

**TERRAIN**: Mountainous. There are good tracks on the lower slopes, with steep and rocky paths on the higher slopes. Care is needed near any cliff faces that may be hidden from view, particularly in mist or poor visibility.

**DIFFICULTY**: Difficult

**PUBLIC TRANSPORT**: Ulsterbus 34 and 34B are infrequent services running close to Trassey. Ulsterbus 405 also passes close to Trassey in the summer.

## THE WALK

Slieve Bearnagh is a remarkable rocky peak, easily recognised in views from all around the Mountains of Mourne. It often seems to stand alone, flanked as it is by deeply cut gaps, and its name translates as the 'Mountain of the Gap'. Slieve Bearnagh's steep slopes appear pyramidal, but its crowning glory is its rocky summit tor. Even when seen from a distance, Slieve Bearnagh's rocky top looks sharp and jagged, and to reach the highest point you will need to use your hands. Alternatively, you may err on the side of caution, viewing the summit tor from a grassy shoulder. The builders of the mighty Mourne Wall had to leave several gaps in their handiwork on Slieve Bearnagh, silent testimony to the steep and rugged slopes of the mountain. A walk over Slieve Bearnagh is easily linked with neighbouring summits simply by following the course of the Mourne Wall.

## THE ROUTE

Leave the Cecil Newman car park and picnic site at Trassey and turn left, heading roughly south up a narrow road. Cross a stone step stile beside a gate to follow the Trassey Track. A metal plaque names the track and offers basic route information. The first part of the track is

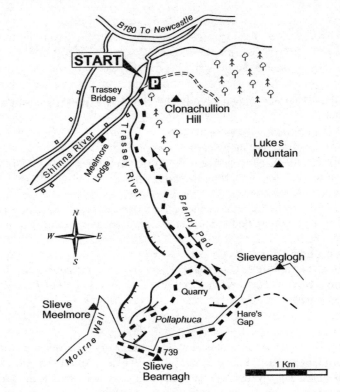

lined with gorse bushes, and then beyond another gate it continues through part of Clonachullion Wood. The stony track later runs with forest to the left and gorse bushes to the right to reach yet another gate, with the Mountains of Mourne rising directly ahead.

Leave the gate at the corner of Clonachullion Wood and follow the Trassey Track gently uphill, noting that it moves gradually closer to the Trassey River as it climbs. Tracks and paths to right and left lead across rugged slopes of heather to reach small, abandoned granite quarries. As soon as the track fords the river, turn right along a narrower track that winds up into a rock-strewn valley. You can see a small quarry higher up the slope, but keep away from it and follow the path further and further up towards the head of the valley, which is called Pollaphuca. The path reaches a gap that is crossed by the Mourne Wall.

Climb a ladder stile over the Mourne Wall and enjoy the view through the gap to Doan and Slieve Muck. Turn left to start climbing the steep slopes of Slieve Bearnagh. The path drifts away from the wall and the wall itself features a gap where its builders were defeated by a steep, slabby rockface. (Take careful note of this rockface if walking in the opposite direction down the slope.) Continue steeply uphill on a bouldery slope beside the wall. At the top, you will realise that the highest part of Slieve Bearnagh is off to the right, where a large granite tor thrusts skywards from a gentle shoulder of short grass. If you wish to climb all the way to the top, you will need to use your hands to scramble over the blocky outcrops, making this one of the toughest Mourne summits to bring underfoot. The altitude is 739m (2394ft). Inaccessible cliffs around Slieve Bearnagh provide good nesting sites for ravens, ensuring that the sky is their preserve. Often, their '*pruck, pruck*' calls will be the only sounds heard on the mountain.

Views from Slieve Bearnagh take in the peak of Ben Crom to the south, the Silent Valley and the sea beyond Kilkeel.Turning clockwise, Slievenaglogh rises above the Silent Valley, with the forested hump of Knockchree beyond, and rugged Doan closer to hand. There is a peep through to Carlingford Lough, with Lough Shannagh seen at the foot of Slieve Muck. The rugged crest of Slieve Foye features distantly, and the nearby Slieve Loughshannagh separates it from its neighbour, Slieve Gullion. Cock Mountain is seen between Slieve Meelbeg and Slieve Meelmore, then the Belfast Hills and Slieve Croob break the distant horizon. Much closer to hand are Slievenaglogh, Slieve Corragh, Slieve Commedagh and Slieve Donard. Between Cove Mountain and Slievelamagan you can see Chimney Rock Mountain, then the North Tor leads the eye to the rugged crest of Slieve Binnian. You can see small stretches of the Ben Crom and Silent Valley Reservoirs, on either side of the rugged little peak of Ben Crom.

The path drifts away from the Mourne Wall to descend from Slieve Bearnagh. A couple of other granite tors cause breaks in the wall, so anyone following its exact course must be prepared for more hands-on scrambling. The path drops steeply on a grassy slope that becomes bouldery. A heathery shoulder bears a few rocky outcrops, then the wall drops steeply downhill again. Beware of a break in the wall, where there is another short, slabby cliff face. Keep well to the right to find a flight of stone steps leading down to a cairn built around a metal post on the Hare's Gap. Note the course of the Brandy Pad, the obvious path running eastwards in the view from the gap.

Go through a gate in the Mourne Wall on Hare's Gap and walk down into the valley. The slope at the head of the valley is bouldery and usually wet. Take care not to turn an ankle on the way down. The path is vague but gets better as it levels out, fording the river and joining a track down from the old quarry noticed earlier in the day's walk. Ford the river again and simply follow the Trassey River and Trassey Track back down the rugged slope and alongside the forest, retracing your earlier steps of the day to return to the Cecil Newman car park. This walk could be restructured to start and finish at Meelmore Lodge, which is only a short way along the Slievenamon Road from the Cecil Newman car park. Meelmore Lodge offers bed and breakfast, campsite and a café, as well as having its own car park for patrons, and its own access to the Mourne Way and Trassey Track. Telephone 028-43726657, website meelmorelodge.co.uk.

Ravens can be seen wheeling in the sky around Slieve Bearnagh.
Large, heavily built members of the crow family, they feed chiefly on carrion.

# WALK 19 – SLIEVE COMMEDAGH FROM TRASSEY

**START**: The Cecil Newman car park at Trassey near Bryansford – 311314.

**DISTANCE**: 14 kilometres (8¾ miles).

**TOTAL ASCENT**: 800 metres (2625 feet).

**MAPS**: OSNI Discoverer Sheet 29. OSNI Mourne Country Outdoor Pursuits Map. Harvey's Mourne Mountains.

**TERRAIN**: Mountainous. There are good paths and tracks on the lower slopes, and the Mourne Wall is a good feature to follow to the top. There is a rough and pathless slope on the descent, followed by clear forest tracks and paths.

**DIFFICULTY**: Difficult

**PUBLIC TRANSPORT**: Ulsterbus 34 and 34B are infrequent services running close to Trassey. Ulsterbus 405 also passes close to Trassey in the summer.

## THE WALK

Slieve Commedagh is one of the best known of the Mountains of Mourne. As a close neighbour of the highest in the range, Slieve Donard, it is generally easy to spot in views. Its grassy dome is a joy to walk across, and the Mourne Wall incorporates a lookout tower close to the summit. There are several ways to climb Slieve Commedagh, and this particular route starts at Trassey. The Trassey Track and Brandy Pad are used to reach the Hare's Gap, then the Mourne Wall is followed over Slievenaglogh and Slieve Corragh to reach the summit of Slieve Commedagh. To return to Trassey, a rough and pathless descent to the Cascade River can be coupled with a walk along forest tracks and paths, following the course of the Mourne Way.

## THE ROUTE

Leave the Cecil Newman car park and picnic site at Trassey and turn left, heading roughly south up a narrow road. Cross a stone step stile beside a gate to follow the Trassey Track. A metal plaque names the track and offers basic route information. The first part of the track is lined with gorse bushes, and then beyond another gate it continues through part of Clonachullion Wood. The stony track later runs with forest to the left and gorse bushes to the right to reach yet another gate, with the Mountains of Mourne rising directly ahead.

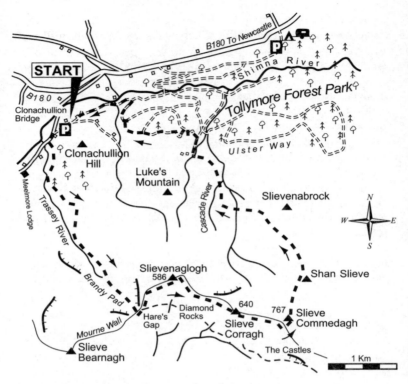

Leave the gate at the corner of Clonachullion Wood and follow the Trassey Track gently uphill, noting that it moves gradually closer to the Trassey River as it climbs. Tracks and paths to right and left lead across rugged slopes of heather to reach small, abandoned granite quarries. The track fords the river, then fords it again as it moves towards the rugged, bouldery head of the glen. The slope at the head of the glen is usually wet and the path can be vague in places. However, by climbing always uphill, you will eventually reach the Mourne Wall, where it crosses the Hare's Gap. Go through a gate in the wall and you will see a cairn built around a metal post.

Turn left to climb up a flight of granite steps. A steep and slabby rock face causes a gap in the course of the Mourne Wall, and this is something you should beware of if you follow this route in the opposite direction in mist or poor visibility. When the wall resumes its course, it is of truly monumental proportions, as there was evidently never any shortage of building material alongside. You can clearly discern 'plug and feather' marks where the blocks were split. There are huge 'footing' stones, several projecting 'through' stones in the middle of the wall, and well-laid 'cam' stones on top of the wall. Walk past a ladder stile on a shoulder of Slievenaglogh and continue gently uphill, walking on short grass or granite slabs close to the wall, with heather and boulders alongside. A large cairn marks the summit, sitting on a granite platform to the right at 586m (1922ft). The name 'Diamond Rocks' on maps refers to a particularly crystalline outcrop of granite.

Continue downhill, following the Mourne Wall across a slight gap, then climb over a subsidiary summit before following the wall down to a slightly lower gap. Climb steadily uphill on the slopes of Slieve Corragh. The summit features low and rounded outcrops of granite at around 640m (2100ft). The wall now turns left and runs downhill a short way, following a steep-sided crest as it crosses another gap. This is actually one of the narrowest ridges in the Mountains of Mourne, but it isn't really apparent as the wall prevents you from seeing both sides of the ridge at the same time. A steep grassy slope needs to be climbed next, and there is a pipe dispensing clear spring water if you need to quench your thirst on the ascent. As the gradient eases you reach a prominent lookout tower whose doorway lintel is carved with the date 1913. This is not quite on the true summit of Slieve Commedagh, but it is perched on a shoulder offering excellent views.

The panorama takes in Slieve Donard, Chimney Rock Mountain and Rocky Mountain, with a peep through to the tiny fields of the Kingdom of Mourne. Turning clockwise, Cove Mountain, Slievelamagan, the North Tor and Slieve Binnian all appear one after the other. Carlingford Lough and Slieve Foye are seen well beyond the Silent Valley, with Ben Crom much closer to hand rising from the valley. Finlieve is far away, with Slieve Muck being closer, and Doan closer still. Distant Slieve Gullion is seen beyond Carn Mountain, then nearby peaks include Slieve Bearnagh and

A section of the Mourne Wall, showing 'footing' stones at its base, 'through' stones projecting from the middle of the wall and 'cam' stones laid on top.

Slieve Meelmore, leading the eye to the Hare's Gap. Slievenaglogh and Slieve Corragh, both recently traversed, are in view below. Slieve Croob and St John's Point are seen beyond the true summit of Slieve Commedagh, which is actually on the other side of the Mourne Wall.

You have to climb over the Mourne Wall to reach the highest point on Slieve Commedagh. A vague path leads across short grass to reach the summit cairn. This sits on the foundations of a larger, older cairn; probably an ancient burial cairn. The altitude is 767m (2512ft). The descent from this point needs care if attempted in mist or poor visibility. There is a faint path along the grassy ridge leading towards the hump of Shan Slieve to the north. You pass another cairn and can enjoy good views down into the glens to either side. Drift to the left to descend north-westwards on a steepening slope of grass. The ground becomes rockier and heathery, with some wet patches further down. Watch carefully to spot the line of a ruined wall, which you should join and turn left to follow. It leads down to the Cascade River, which flows through a rugged gully. Clamber into the gully and ford the river, then climb up the other side and continue to follow the wall around a corner. A wet and boggy slope bears plenty of bog myrtle, but there are also drier areas covered in bracken and gorse. Turn left at the bottom of the slope and pass an old gateway to reach an old cottage at the foot of Luke's Mountain.

Walk downhill from the cottage along an old track and cross a ladder stile beside a gate to enter Tollymore Forest. Walk down the track and turn left at a junction. The forest track zig-zags uphill and you should keep left at a junction with another track to continue climbing. When the track descends, it turns right near the edge of the forest, and you should cut off to the left down a path. Turn right at the bottom, then left and let the path lead you down alongside a river to a junction with other tracks. Turn left to follow the Mourne Way across Maria's Bridge and admire a slender waterfall. The track rises gently and passes the Salmon Leap viewpoint. The track reaches the edge of the forest, crossing a ladder stile beside a gate. A muddy stretch of track leads to a stone step stile beside another gate, and finally to another ladder stile beside one last gate. Follow the farm access track onwards to reach a narrow tarmac road. Turn right to return to the Cecil Newman car park where the walk started. This walk could also start and finish at Meelmore Lodge, which offers bed and breakfast, campsite and a café. Telephone 028-43726657, website meelmorelodge.co.uk.

# WALK 20 – SLIEVE COMMEDAGH FROM NEWCASTLE

**START**: Donard Park at Newcastle – 375306.

**DISTANCE**: 14 kilometres (8¾ miles).

**TOTAL ASCENT**: 800 metres (2625 feet).

**MAPS**: OSNI Discoverer Sheet 29. OSNI Mourne Country Outdoor Pursuits Map. Harvey's Mourne Mountains.

**TERRAIN**: Mountainous. There are plenty of paths and tracks on the lower slopes and on the forested foothills. There is a rough and pathless stretch on the ascent, and then good paths are used for the descent.

**DIFFICULTY**: Difficult

**PUBLIC TRANSPORT**: Several Ulsterbus services serve Newcastle, including 17, 17A, 18, 20, 26B, 32, 34, 34B, 36, 37 and, in summer, 405.

## THE WALK

Slieve Commedagh is a high, domed mountain rising high above Newcastle, with lofty Slieve Donard as its nearest neighbour. The Mourne Wall crosses the mountain and most walkers are content to follow its course. The northern slopes of Slieve Commedagh are quite barren and virtually pathless, though the lower slopes are quite well forested. There are several ways to bring the summit underfoot, and this particular route starts by following the Mourne Way out of Newcastle. After making an ascent on a pathless slope, the Mourne Wall and the Glen River Path are used to lead you back down to Newcastle.

## THE ROUTE

Donard Park is on the southern side of Newcastle. There is a large car park beside sports pitches, with toilets and the Central Park bar and restaurant immediately to hand. Leave the car park and walk along Newcastle's sea front. There are promenade paths leading along a green strip, continuing between a bouldery embankment and the Tropicana centre. When you reach a river, cross over the road and head inland through Castle Park opposite the library, following Mourne Way signposts. There is a boating pool and children's play area, with an exit leading onto the busy Bryansford Road. Cross the road to pick up another path and cross two footbridges over rivers. A tarmac path runs

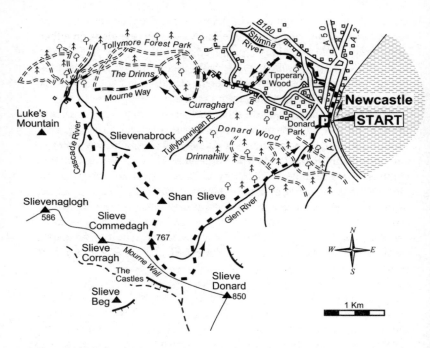

upstream alongside the Shimna River, passing grassy areas and fine trees. Turn left and cross a road bridge over the river, then turn right to enter Tipperary Wood. Another riverside path continues upstream, through a gate, then a gravel track called Tipperary Lane leads past Tipperary House and up to a narrow tarmac road.

Turn right to walk up the road, then turn left up a narrower road. Go through a gate at the end of the road and cross a wooden step stile beside another gate. A forest track zigzags uphill and you turn left at a junction of tracks to rise more gently around the forested slopes of Curraghard. There are fine views across Newcastle, Murlough and Dundrum Bay to St John's Point. Keep left at the next junction of tracks, following a track close to the edge of the forest at the Drinns, where there is a fine mixture of trees. There is a view of rugged slopes to the left, and you will later see a small gate on the left allowing you to reach these slopes. Head roughly southwards, aiming for a gap between a rounded hill close to the forest and the much larger Slievenabrock further away. The ground is rough and wet underfoot, and eventually you reach the course of a ruined dry stone wall. Step through one of the gaps and start climbing more steeply. Although the slope is rocky and wet in places, there is drier heather and grass as height is gained. There is a cairn on top of Shan Slieve, where there are fine views into the glens on either side. Simply continue along a path leading up the grassy ridge to the summit of Slieve Commedagh. A cairn sits on the foundations of a larger, older cairn; probably an ancient burial cairn. The altitude is 767m (2512ft) and the whole summit area is covered in short grass.

Views are quite extensive from the summit, but to experience a greater sense of depth you should continue over the broad, grassy summit to reach a prominent lookout tower whose doorway lintel is carved with the date 1913. The panorama takes in Slieve Donard, Chimney Rock Mountain and Rocky Mountain, with a peep through to the tiny fields of the Kingdom of Mourne. Turning clockwise, Cove Mountain, Slievelamagan, the North Tor and Slieve Binnian all appear one after the other. Carlingford Lough and Slieve Foye are seen well beyond the Silent Valley, with Ben Crom much closer to hand rising from the valley. Finlieve is far away, with Slieve Muck being closer, and Doan closer still. Distant Slieve Gullion is seen beyond Carn Mountain, then nearby peaks include Slieve Bearnagh and Slieve Meelmore, leading the eye to the Hare's Gap. Slievenaglogh and Slieve Corragh are in view below. Slieve Croob and St John's Point are seen beyond the true summit of Slieve Commedagh.

Don't cross the Mourne Wall, but turn left and follow it downhill. A steep, grassy slope gives way to a level shoulder, then another steep grassy slope leads down to a broad gap, with Slieve Donard looming ahead. You could of course continue onwards to climb Slieve Donard if you wish, otherwise turn left to leave the wall and descend from the gap. Pass a large cairn and link with the reconstructed Glen River Path. Built like a stairway of granite, the path descends in a broad loop around the head of the glen and crosses the Glen River below. Stay on the reconstructed path to avoid causing unnecessary erosion on the fragile boggy ground alongside. The path is quite bouldery by the time it runs alongside a forest. Across the river is a domed stone structure which is a restored ice house – an eighteenth-century domestic freezer for the now demolished Donard Lodge!

Go through a gate and follow a rugged path down to a forest track, which you cross to continue downstream through Donard Forest. The forest has been developed around the former Donard Demesne and covers an area of 280 hectares (690 acres). There are attractive pines, firs and larches alongside the river, and great slabs of granite are exposed in the riverbed, with large blocks alongside. The bedrock later

The leaves, fruit and buds of (from the top): rowan, birch, oak, sweet chestnut and beech.

changes to ancient sandstones and mudstones, shot through with igneous dykes, and the river is confined to a narrower gorge. When you reach a bridge, turn right to cross it, then turn left and continue downstream. The rough and rocky path passes slender waterfalls in an undercut gorge, then steps lead down onto a rugged track. Turn left to cross Donard Bridge, a granite arch built in 1835. Turn right and continue downstream beside the Glen River. The riverside path leads down through a wonderfully mixed woodland featuring oak, beech, birch, sweet chestnut, rowan, holly and ivy. The woodland was once part of Donard Demesne. Donard Lodge, built in the 1830s by the Annesley family, was finally demolished in 1966 after falling into ruin. The path broadens to become a track, passing through two gates to return to the car park at Donard Park.

# WALK 21 - SLIEVE DONARD FROM NEWCASTLE

**START**: Donard Park at Newcastle – 375306.

**DISTANCE**: 15 kilometres (9¼ miles).

**TOTAL ASCENT**: 1000 metres (3280 feet).

**MAPS**: OSNI Discoverer Sheet 29. OSNI Mourne Country Outdoor Pursuits Map. Harvey's Mourne Mountains.

**TERRAIN**: Mountainous. Good paths and tracks for most of the walk, but the slopes are often quite steep, and can be rough and bouldery in places.

**DIFFICULTY**: Difficult

**PUBLIC TRANSPORT**: Several Ulsterbus services converge on Newcastle, including 17, 17A, 18, 20, 26B, 32, 34, 34B, 36, 37 and, in summer, 405.

## THE WALK

Slieve Donard is the highest of the Mountains of Mourne, and indeed is the highest mountain in the Province of Ulster. It was known in ancient times as Sliabh Slainge, after one Slanga, son of Partholan, who came to Ireland after the Battle of Troy. In early Christian times the summit of the mountain was frequented by St Domangard, a disciple of St Patrick, and so became known as Sliabh Domangard, and ultimately Slieve Donard. In 1991 Slieve Donard and neighbouring Slieve Commedagh were purchased by the National Trust for half a million pounds. As an ever-present backdrop to the seaside resort of Newcastle, Slieve Donard attracts thousands of people to its slopes, though not all of them reach the summit! The usual route to the top starts at Donard Park and follows the Glen River up through Donard Forest. This popular path has been extensively repaired towards the head of the glen, conveying walkers to the Mourne Wall. The course of the wall is then used to make a direct ascent to the summit of Slieve Donard. While many walkers are happy to retrace their steps, it is also possible to make a circuit by following the Bloody Bridge River down to the coast, then link with tracks in Donard Forest to return to Donard Park.

## THE ROUTE

Donard Park is on the southern side of Newcastle. There is a large car park beside sports pitches, with toilets and O'Hare's café bar close to

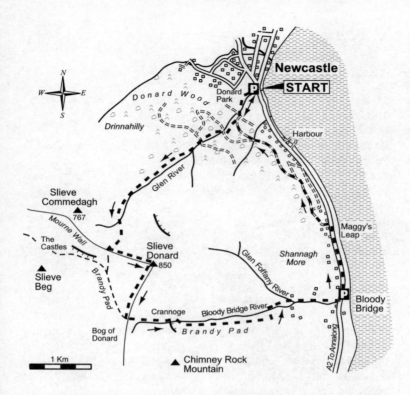

hand. Walk through the car park and go through two gates to find
yourself on a broad track beside the Glen River. The river is screened
from view by trees and bushes, but you can hear the water. The track
narrows to a path and a sign announces that you are entering Donard
Forest. Follow the riverside path uphill through wonderfully mixed
woodland, featuring oak, beech, birch, sweet chestnut, rowan, holly
and ivy. The woodland was once part of Donard Demesne. Donard
Lodge, which was built in the 1830s by the Annesley family, eventually
fell into ruin and was demolished in 1966. Donard Forest has been
developed around the former demesne and covers an area of 280
hectares (690 acres).

Turn left to cross Donard Bridge, a granite arch that was built in
1835. Turn right to continue upstream beside the Glen River, following
a rough and stony track. Steps lead up to a narrower path, rough and
rocky in places, and sometimes worn down to bare rock. The river often

The Glen River Path rises ruggedly from Donard Forest.

flows in an undercut rocky gorge, carved from sandstones and mudstones shot through with igneous dykes. There is quite a variety of trees beside the river, and the forested slopes nearby contain a mixture of pines, firs and larches. When another bridge is reached, turn right to cross it, then turn left to continue upstream on another rough riverside path. The rock changes to granite, with great slabs of it in the riverbed and large blocks lying alongside in the forest. Cross a forest track near a concrete bridge and walk further up the rugged path. Go through a gate to see the wilder upper reaches of the Glen River.

The path proceeds, rough and bouldery, on the ground between the forest fence and the Glen River. Across the river is a domed stone structure which is a restored ice house – an eighteenth-century domestic freezer for Donard Lodge! As you work your way through the bouldery head of the glen, notice how parts of the path have been crazy-paved with granite slabs. This is not to make the way easy, but to prevent serious erosion to the surrounding mountainside, so please be sure to walk on these restored stretches. The path leads across the Glen River, then rising like a stone stairway curves up the steep slope to reach a prominent gap, between Slieve Commedagh to the right and Slieve Donard to the left. There is a large cairn on the gap, but the most arresting feature is the course of the Mourne Wall sweeping down from one summit, across the gap, and up the other summit. There is a double stone step stile over the wall, but you don't need to cross it. The view from the gap takes in Rocky Mountain to the south, the heathery Annalong Valley and the distant fields of the Kingdom of Mourne beyond. Slieve Binnian's rugged crest is followed by the smoother slopes of Slievelamagan and Cove Mountain to the south-west.

Turn left to follow the Mourne Wall uphill from the gap. The slope is steep and grassy, with some small embedded boulders in places. The gradient is unremitting and it is not possible to see the summit until you are almost there. At the top, a prominent stone lookout tower, whose lintel is carved with the date 1910, sits cosily in a corner of the Mourne Wall. A trig point has been mounted on top of the tower, at an altitude of 850m (2796ft). There is a large cairn beside the wall, called the Great Carn, while a short walk along a grassy path to a bouldery slope overlooking Newcastle leads you to another cairn known as the Lesser Carn. The Lesser Carn may well be an ancient burial cairn, while the Great Carn may contain stones that were once part of St Domangard's mountain-top oratory.

Views from the summit of Slieve Donard are of course very extensive, and in clear weather can extend far beyond the Mountains of Mourne to the Wicklow Mountains beyond Dublin, to Co Antrim and the Galloway Hills of Scotland, and out to sea to the Isle of Man. A more usual view would comprise the following features: neighbouring Chimney Rock Mountain and Rocky Mountain, roughly to the south, giving way to the farmlands of the Kingdom of Mourne and the mouth of Carlingford Lough. Turning clockwise, Slieve Binnian's rugged crest gives way to a distant view of Slieve Foye and Slieve Martin, before the North Tor rises closer to hand. Beyond Slievelamagan, the Cooley Hills, Eagle Mountain and Slieve Muck can be seen. Cove Mountain and Doan lead the eye to Carn Mountain and distant Slieve Gullion. After nearby Slieve Beg come Slieve Loughshannagh, Slieve Meelbeg, rugged Slieve Bearnagh, Slieve Meelmore and the Hare's Gap. Slieve Commedagh is close to Slieve Donard, but there are also distant views of Slieve Croob, Dundrum Bay and St John's Point.

Follow the Mourne Wall steeply down the southern slopes of Slieve Donard. It is best to cross a stone step stile on the summit, then walk on the western side of the wall, on the same side as the Annalong Valley, for the best ground conditions underfoot. The slope is steep and grassy, with a few rashes of embedded boulders. Rugged heather slopes close in on the wall before it levels out on the Bog of Donard.

At the bottom, cross a stone step stile back over the wall and follow a broad, clear path eastwards as it slices through the surrounding heather. The path becomes braided and bouldery as it follows the headwaters of the Bloody Bridge River downstream. The rugged track swings left and right as it passes a granite quarry and its associated spoils, seen across the river. The track is usually in a stony groove, but is sometimes grassy. Ford the Bloody Bridge River, climb a short way uphill, then turn left along the broad and stony track that runs downhill from the old quarry. The track has some pronounced bends, and then there is a left turn down a fenced track leading to the river, which needs to be forded again. (If the Bloody Bridge River is in spate and you cannot ford it, you can stay on the northern bank the whole time.) The river below the ford features great slabs of granite. Follow a bouldery path downstream and cross a wooden step stile at a point where two large water pipelines cross the river. The bouldery path leads to a footbridge over the Glen Fofanny River, and then the path improves as it continues between banks of gorse. The old Bloody Bridge lies off to the right, a single stone arch over the Bloody Bridge River. It was the scene of a massacre in 1641, when the Magennises ambushed a band of Presbyterian prisoners being led between jails in Newry and Newcastle. The modern bridge carries the main A2 coast road a little further downstream. The path goes though a wooden squeeze stile and a small gate to reach the main road. Take care at this point, as the traffic is fast. Cross the road and turn left to reach a car park and toilet block.

Follow the road northwards, back towards Newcastle. There isn't a footway, so walk on the right, facing the traffic. Continue past the mixed woodland surrounding the Shannagh-More Outdoor Education Centre. Watch for a rocky cleft to the right later, on private property, known as Maggy's Leap. It seems that Maggy was a local girl who leapt across the chasm to escape a persistent suitor! When a sign welcoming visitors to Down District appears by the roadside, turn left up a road signposted as private. The narrow road runs uphill and turns right to cross a stream called Srupatrick to reach a gate and wooden step stile giving access to Donard Forest. Walk up the forest track, over a crest, then turn left at a junction. The track runs downhill and crosses a bridge over a small stream. There is a glimpse to the right of Newcastle's tiny harbour. Follow the track onwards and turn right at the next junction, crossing a narrow ravine. The track runs gently downhill and there is a small stone shelter to the left, known as The Grotto, one of several little follies built around the Donard Demesne. There is a much greater variety of trees along the way now. When a barrier gate is reached, turn right down a rough track that was used earlier in the day's walk. Turn left across Donard Bridge, then turn right downhill alongside the Glen River to return to Donard Park.

It might be worth bearing in mind a variety of short waymarked trails in Donard Forest. There are three loops available, all marked by colour-coded arrows – yellow arrows mark the central loop called the Pinewood Trail; blue arrows mark the western loop called the Contour Trail; and white arrows mark the eastern loop, the Drinahilly Trail.

# WALK 22 - TOLLYMORE FOREST PARK

**START:** At the Bryansford Gate entrance to Tollymore – 345328.
**DISTANCE:** 9 kilometres (5½ miles).
**TOTAL ASCENT:** 200 metres (655 feet).
**MAPS:** OSNI Discoverer Sheet 29. OSNI Mourne Country Outdoor Pursuits Map. OSNI 1:10,000 Tollymore Forest Park Map. Tollymore Forest Park Forest Trails Map. Harvey's Mourne Mountains.
**TERRAIN:** Forested riversides. There are plenty of good, clear, firm, well-waymarked forest tracks and paths.
**DIFFICULTY:** Easy
**PUBLIC TRANSPORT:** Ulsterbus 34 and 34B serve the Bryansford Gate from Newcastle and, in summer, also Ulsterbus 405.

## THE WALK

Visitors have enjoyed the woodlands at Tollymore since the early eighteenth century. The area measures 500 hectares (1235 acres) and has been managed and planted as a forest since 1930. In 1955 it was the first forest in Northern Ireland to be designated a Forest Park. There is a wealth of tree species, not only in the commercial plantings, but also in a series of square plots, and arranged in an interesting arboretum. The rivers draining the forest are quite charming, with numerous small waterfalls and cascades. There are also small lakes and ponds that attract a variety of waterfowl. The varied habitats within the forest have attracted up to eighty species of birds. The forest is also home to occasional otters and the elusive pine marten. To assist walkers exploring the Forest Park, a series of colour-coded waymarked forest trails have been established, and a combination of these trails is offered below. You can obtain a leaflet showing the layout of these trails from the information kiosk.

## THE ROUTE

There are two main entry points to the Tollymore Forest Park – the Barbican Gate and the Bryansford Gate. Entry via the Barbican Gate leads you along an avenue of

The shy and elusive Pine Marten.

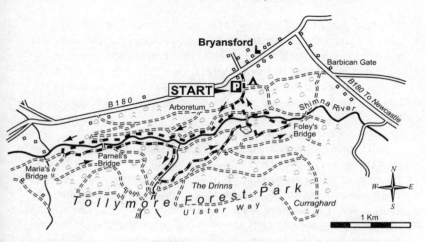

bizarre Himalayan cedars. Entry via the Bryansford Gate leads straight past the Clanbrassil Barn, which contains displays relating to the history, heritage, flora and fauna of the Forest Park. The 'barn' was built around 1757 as a stables and store, and looks remarkably like a country church. Bus services pass both gates while running from Newcastle to Bryansford, while motorists should use one of the large car parks near the Clanbrassil Barn. There is also an information kiosk, toilets, and information boards showing the layout of a series of colour-coded, waymarked forest trails. A combination of these trails allows a varied and interesting exploration of the Forest Park, particularly of its rivers, waterfalls and ponds.

Check the information board at the lower car park. The blue arrows of the Rivers Trail are followed for most of this walk, ending with a loop marked by the yellow arrows of the Lakes and Ponds Trail. There is an option, after returning to this car park, to follow the white arrows marking the Arboretum and Forest Plots Trail. Turn right to walk away from the board, then turn left downhill, following the blue arrows on marker posts. A tarmac path leads down through exotic shrubberies, then passes beneath a stone arch. The path splits to run on both sides of a tumbling stream, joining together again further downhill. The tarmac ends at a junction with a forest track, but you simply cross over and follow a gravel path down to the Shimna River.

Turn right as indicated by a blue arrow, also signposted for Parnell's Bridge, to follow a path upstream alongside the Shimna River. The woodlands beside the river are delightfully mixed. Pass a footbridge called the Footstick. Don't cross it, but maybe use it to view the rocky gorge where the flow of the river has been determined by the near-vertical Silurian strata forming the bedrock. The path continues upstream to reach the Hermitage. This is a curious structure comprising a number of crude stone rooms overlooking a deep and tranquil part of the river. It seems to cling to a cliff face and at the furthest point you have a view of a waterfall. James Hamilton, 2nd Earl of Clanbrassil, built the Hermitage in memory of his friend the Marquis of Momthermer, who died in 1770.

There are some tall and stately beeches alongside the river as the path proceeds upstream. You will notice a set of stepping stones across the river, and there are more stepping stones further upstream, then you reach the Meeting of the Waters, where the Cascade River joins the Shimna River. Further upstream, a fine mossy oak clings to an undercut bank and must surely one day topple into the river. The Rustic Bridge is a wooden footbridge spanning the river, followed by a shelter, then the path moves between the river and a stand of mature conifers. A series of cascades in the river can be enjoyed, then you will notice yet another set of stepping stones. The path enters another area of mixed woodlands before reaching the substantial stone arch of Parnell's Bridge. The bridge is named after Sir John Parnell, the great grandfather of Charles Stewart Parnell, the 'uncrowned king of Ireland'.

Although there is a blue arrow pointing across the bridge, it is worth continuing upstream a little further to reach the tumbled wall marking the boundary of the forest. Cross the wooden Boundary Bridge over the Shimna River and continue along a path passing some young trees. There are areas of wood sorrel and woodrush where more light reaches the ground. The path swings uphill to the left to reach a junction with forest tracks. You could make a diversion to the right to reach Maria's Bridge, where there is a close-up view of a fine little waterfall. To continue, however, you should turn left as signposted along the forest track for Parnell's Bridge.

By walking straight past the bridge you will again be following the blue waymark arrows. The track rises gently, then there is a left turn down another track. You will pass a set of stepping stones, as well as the Rustic Bridge again, to enter a stand of tall conifers. The track drifts away from the river to reach a clearing, where there is a curious arrangement of two bridges at a junction of tracks. Turn right uphill along the track signposted 'Cascade'. This track runs parallel to the Cascade River, following it upstream from Altavaddy Bridge, with Luke's Mountain rising ahead. There is a lovely gorge to the left, but it is not always easy to see into it. When you reach a shelter, however, there is a fenced path and steps to the left allowing access to the gorge, where you can admire a small waterfall. Continuing up the path, you pass some fine oaks, then turn left to cross the wooden Spinkwee Bridge. A path climbs uphill and you turn left along a track amid tall conifers. Follow the track down into a dip where tall beech trees predominate, then walk uphill again. At a track junction just before a corrugated hut, turn left downhill as signposted for the Old Bridge. The track runs down through an area of beeches mixed with conifers, then at the next junction you turn right, as signposted for a lake. Follow the lakeshore path, which has picnic tables and a shelter. You should be able to spot mallard, Muscovy ducks and moorhens. Waterfowl use the artificial wooded islets in the lake for refuge.

Switch to following the yellow markers of the Lakes and Ponds Trail and turn right to cross the dam. Walk across a footbridge over the outflowing stream and turn left, then left again along a track. After passing some tall beech trees, turn left as marked by a yellow arrow and cross a footbridge beside a mighty oak tree. Follow a path and track downstream in mixed mature woodland, then cross the stream again to continue. You will notice two small millponds off to the left, and you turn left to cross the dam on the lower pond. A path swings round a slope to follow the Shimna River upstream. Cross over the graceful stone span of Foley's bridge, which was built in 1787. Note the curious projecting boulders of granite on the arch. Turn left to continue upstream along a broader track. A huge boulder on the right has the following words carved on it: 'Stop. Look around and praise the Name of Him who made it all. See 1$^{st}$ chp Iohn 3 verse.' The track leads onwards to the Old Bridge, which was built in 1726 and repaired in 1822. From the bridge you can see fine cascades in the rocky gorge. Off to the right is a path marked with yellow, red and blue arrows, where the waymarked forest trails climb back up to the car park.

If you have time to spare afterwards, it is worth following the white arrows of the Arboretum and Forest Plots Trail. This is a well-waymarked route along tracks, paths and grassy rides. The forest plots are seen first, where square blocks have been planted with a variety of trees. The Arboretum comes later, where individual specimens of dozens of trees have been planted on spacious lawns. You can admire ghostly pale eucalyptus, contorted Chile pines, larches, cedars, hornbeams, maples, birches and a rather curious gnarled cork tree. The trail leads in a circuit returning to the car park.

# WALK 23 - MURLOUGH NATIONAL NATURE RESERVE

**START**: Beside Main Street, south of Dundrum - 402361.
**DISTANCE**: 10 kilometres (6 miles).
**TOTAL ASCENT**: 30 metres (100 feet).
**MAPS**: OSNI Discoverer Sheets 21 and 29. OSNI Mourne Country Outdoor Pursuits Map.
**TERRAIN**: Coastal walking. Good paths and tracks are used, as well as beach walking. Very high tides can be a problem for a short time on the beaches.
**DIFFICULTY**: Easy
**PUBLIC TRANSPORT**: Ulsterbus services 17 and 20 link Dundrum with Newcastle.

## THE WALK

While this walk may seem rather removed from the Mountains of Mourne, traversing sand dunes that are barely above sea level, it does include some striking views of the mountains. The Murlough Dunes are owned by the National Trust and have been managed since 1967 as Ireland's first nature reserve. There are a variety of habitats, including the open sea and the more enclosed Dundrum Inner Bay; flowery heaths; woody scrub; and sand and shingle beaches. The Murlough National Nature Reserve combines all these habitats in some 282 hectares (696 acres) and supports a rich and varied collection of flora and fauna. In the summer months the heathlands are ablaze with flowers, while the autumn crop of berries in the woody scrub attracts a variety of birds. The sheltered mudflats are an important wintering ground for ducks and waders, with the sound of piping curlews, while colonies of seals can be observed out in the open bay. Whatever time of year Murlough is visited, you can be sure to find something interesting.

## THE ROUTE

Start by following Main Street from Dundrum, in the direction of Newcastle. On the outskirts of the village, on the left, is a signpost for the Lecale Way, where a small roadside lay-by can be used for parking. Alternatively, bus services stop at a nearby road junction for Keel Point. Follow a grassy shoreline path that joins the road on Keel Point leading

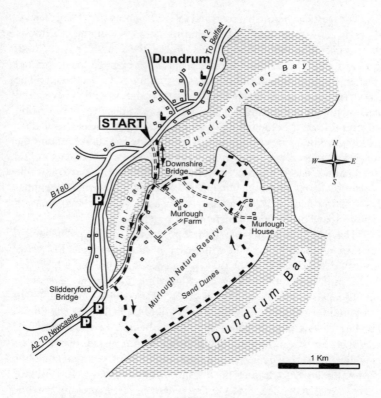

to the Downshire Bridge. There is another small car park on the right just as you reach the bridge, as well as a sign for the Murlough National Nature Reserve. The route so far has actually been on the old trackbed of the railway that once ran between Dundrum and Newcastle. The bridge was built in 1874 and has three spans through which the tide surges with considerable force.

Cross Downshire Bridge and note the sea buckthorn growing profusely alongside, which is an abiding feature of this walk. The autumn crops of golden berries are eagerly devoured by a variety of finches and thrushes. Turn right along a gravel track, sometimes fringed with sea campion, that runs beside Dundrum Inner Bay, where tidal mudflats are often probed by oystercatchers and provide a sheltered area for wintering wildfowl, such as Brent geese. The track passes a couple of houses before joining the main A2 coastal road at an old gatehouse near Slidderyford Bridge, but you don't actually go as far as the road.

Turn left just before the road and follow a pebbly path to a gateway. There is an information board offering notes about the Murlough Dunes, and a wooden walkway leads through the dunes to protect them from erosion. There is an ongoing program to manage the scrub and bracken, control erosion and enhance the quality of the heathlands. The grassy areas are home to rabbits, foxes and badgers, with skylarks and meadow pipits being common. Shelduck sometimes nest in old rabbit burrows. Flowers include bird's-foot trefoil and wild pansies, as well as the less common viper's bugloss and bee orchid. The stable areas of the dunes are often damp enough to support mosses and lichens, while other parts are dry enough for heather to grow. As you follow the wooden walkway onwards, turn left at a yellow post bearing the number 2, and follow another walkway through dunes covered in spiky marram grass to reach a sand and shingle storm beach.

There is a white concrete marker post above the storm beach, and you turn left to walk along the shingle bank at high water. At low water you could walk along the broad sands instead. If you find a high tide causes problems, then look out for other white marker posts, with the top parts painted black, yellow or green. These mark points at which you could head inland and join a network of paths behind the dunes. The beach walk is interesting, as you may be able to see common or grey seals out to sea. There is also a chance to spot various diving birds, as well as wintering duck. As you approach an inlet, you will see a line of prominent signs warning of a military firing range, which is situated in the dunes over near Ballykinler. There is no danger for anyone walking round the Murlough Dunes, and after you pass the third of these signs, you will notice a gap in the dune belt just before reaching a slope covered in wind-blasted trees. Lying not far from the shore, unseen and a hazard to shipping, is the notorious Dundrum Bar. Many ships have run aground on this bar, from an entire fleet of Norse longships in the tenth century to the SS *Great Britain* in 1846.

Head inland along a sandy path flanked by sea buckthorn, brambles and burnet rose. Watch for fieldfare and redwing in this scrubby habitat. The path passes some attractive mixed woodland in which pines are dominant. When you reach a road, cross over and follow a grassy track, keeping to the right at a fork. There are some tall gorse bushes that may favour reed buntings and stonechat. Hazel scrub in this area may attract whitethroat and willow warblers. Patchy mixed woodland is passed by the grassy track, and you should avoid turnings to left and right. There are views of the inlet leading into Dundrum

Inner Bay, as well as to the village of Dundrum, with Slieve Croob far behind. There is a sudden left turn and the grassy track wanders away from the sea, through an expanse of bracken dotted with odd trees and gorse bushes. The Mountains of Mourne rise far beyond, dominated by the domes of Slieve Donard and Slieve Commedagh.

The grassy path approaches a road, which you could join and turn right to follow it. Alternatively, you could turn right beforehand and follow another grassy path marked by blue posts. This is used by horse-riders and can be muddy in places. It runs through a wooded area and continues alongside the road. The road runs through an avenue of trees and the bridleway runs along a parallel avenue. The road passes a gateway beside a gatehouse, then swings right to lead you back across Downshire Bridge again. You can keep to the right of the road to follow a grassy strip, then follow a grassy path back towards Dundrum.

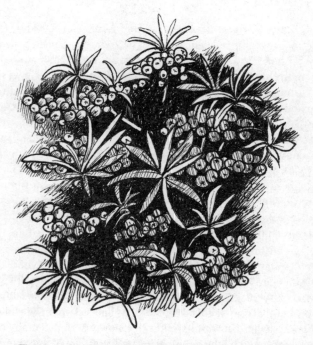

The bushy sea buckthorn displays golden berries in the autumn.

# WALK 24 –
# THE CASTLEWELLAN LOANANS

**START**: At the library in the Upper Square at Castlewellan – 342363.
**DISTANCE**: 18 kilometres (11 miles).
**TOTAL ASCENT**: 230 metres (750 feet).
**MAPS**: OSNI Discoverer Sheet 29. OSNI Slieve Croob Outdoor Pursuits Map.
**TERRAIN**: Low level farmland, with good paths, tracks and roads. Some parts can be quite muddy and may also be used by horse-riders.
**DIFFICULTY**: Easy
**PUBLIC TRANSPORT**: Castlewellan is served by Ulsterbus 17A, 18, 32 and 518 from points such as Newcastle, Downpatrick, Belfast, Ballynahinch and Banbridge.

## THE WALK

Castlewellan owes its street plan to William Annesley, who bought the village in 1741 and redeveloped it. The old courthouse is now the library, built in 1764 with a clock tower added later that tends to make it look more like an old church. A number of old laneways and field paths around Castlewellan have been cleared, improved and signposted by Down District Council as public footpaths and bridleways. They form a network that connect with main roads and minor roads, offering walks where you can leave the tarmac and cut across country away from the traffic. There are two loops which can be linked together to form a satisfying day's walk; one around Drumee and Maghera, and the other around Burrenreagh and Burrenbridge. The bridleways are used first, to reach Maghera Old Church and Round Tower. The footpaths are used afterwards to explore the quiet countryside around Burrenreagh.

## THE ROUTE

Castlewellan Library is an imposing white building in the Upper Square. There is a large car park and a toilet block near the library, as well as plenty of places offering food and drink. Leave the square by following Circular Road to Bunkers Hill and continuing straight on to Drumee Road. The road runs down into a dip and there is a view of the Mountains of Mourne off to the right. The road narrows as it runs

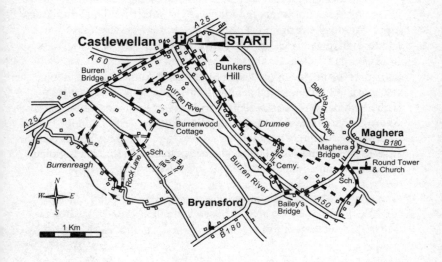

straight onwards, climbing to pass a few houses. The tarmac ends at a house, where a footpath and bridleway signpost points left.

Follow the walled track as it rises and turns right, running between stout dry stone walls as much as two metres (two yards) thick in places. The walls have been formed by gathering together rocks and boulders from the glacial till that covers the land. The fields are seldom ploughed, being used to pasture sheep, cattle and horses. The narrow track is a bridleway, and the surface can be muddy after wet weather. Follow it over a rise between banks of gorse and brambles, then walk down past a house and continue straight along a wider track. As you approach the next house there are belts of tall trees, and you should head off to the left along a narrow walled path. Again, it can be muddy underfoot, and there is another stretch hemmed in by gorse and brambles on the way down between fields. Watch for stout iron gateways either side of the path, which mark the course of an underground water pipeline from the Silent Valley to Belfast. Continue downhill and turn left at a small building, rising gently uphill a short way, then turn right and walk downhill. There are banks of gorse, brambles, bracken, old hedgerows and walls. Some parts are muddy, but the track quickly reaches a firm footing where it joins the Carnacavill Road near St Joseph's Primary School.

Turn left along the road, and either walk straight onwards to the village of Maghera, where the Maghera Inn offers food and drink, or turn right along Corrigs Road as signposted for Maghera Old Church and Round Tower. A green gate on the left reveals the driveway to the little Church of Ireland building. The ruins of a much earlier church lie behind, in an old graveyard, while off to the left is the stump of a round tower in a field. This is all that remains of a small monastery associated with St Domangard, a fifth-century follower of St Patrick, from whom Slieve Donard derives its name.

Walk back along the church drive and turn left along Corrigs Road to pass the Glebe House and Maghera Orange Hall. Turn right up

The stump of St Domangard's round tower, near Maghera church.

Church Hill Road, rising over a crest where fuchsia grows behind a whitewashed wall. As the road runs downhill, turn right along a track signposted as a footpath and bridleway. This is Smiley's Loanan, and as you pass a farmyard complex, the track narrows and is quite muddy. Trees flank it at first, and brambles and ivy later engulf its walls as it rises between fields. Turn left along Carnacavill Road, then right along the busy Newcastle Road. Cross over the road and follow Ballyhafry Road downhill. Turn right up Sawmill Road, then left along the busy Newcastle Road again. Cross over the road to reach the Drumee Cemetery, where there are two footpath and bridleway signposts. Follow the grassy path to the right, which rises between trees, brambly hedges and walls. It joins the end of the Drumee Road, which can be followed straight back towards Castlewellan, or you can enjoy another loop walk as follows:

Turn left down Circular Road and cross the busy Newcastle Road, then continue along Burrenwood Road through a housing estate. At the bottom of the road, walk straight down the grassy Cow Lane, where the walls alongside are rampant with brambles and ivy. Cross a wooden step stile at the bottom of Cow Lane and cross a soft and squelchy field corner to reach a footbridge over the Burren River. Drift right after crossing the bridge, then turn left to cross another footbridge over a drainage ditch. Walk straight up a field and cross a stone step stile beside a gate, then turn left along the Lower Burren Road.

Follow the Lower Burren Road, then turn right up a tree-lined farm track signposted as a public footpath. Walk straight uphill from a junction of tracks, and the stony surface becomes grassy by the time the Upper Burren Road is reached. Turn right along this road and follow until another farm track on the left is signposted as a public footpath. Posts on either side of this track are liberally covered in the number 25! The gravel track is called the Rock Lane and it leads to a house on the brow of a hill. Pass in front of the house using a grassy track, and then pass between another house and a large corrugated barn. The track swings to the right and is flanked by low walls as it crosses over a rise, with fine views of the Mountains of Mourne ahead. The track then runs downhill between gorse bushes to reach the Burren Road close to a derelict farmhouse.

Turn right to follow the Burren Road, and turn right again when another public footpath signpost points along an enclosed farm access track. The track rises gently between fields, but you don't follow it up to the farm. Turn left as marked along a grassy track called Caskell Lane, which rises between more fields and features a fine view of Castlewellan ahead. Walk downhill and turn left along the Burrenreagh Road. This drops down to the busy main A25 road. Turn right to follow this road straight back towards Castlewellan. There is a dip in the road, where you will find the Bridge Bar. The road rises to Castlewellan, passing the prominent spire of St Malachy's Roman Catholic church. Pass through the Lower Square, with its fine oak trees and greens, to return to the Upper Square and the library.

# WALK 25 - CASTLEWELLAN FOREST PARK

**START**: At the library in the Upper Square at Castlewellan – 342363.

**DISTANCE**: 11 kilometres (7 miles).

**TOTAL ASCENT**: 300 metres (985 feet).

**MAPS**: OSNI Discoverer Sheet 29. OSNI Slieve Croob Outdoor Pursuits Map. OSNI 1:10,000 Castlewellan Forest Park Map. Castlewellan Forest Park Forest Trails Map.

**TERRAIN**: Forested hills. The whole walk is accomplished on dry, firm gravel tracks and paths. Most of the paths and tracks are waymarked.

**DIFFICULTY**: Easy

**PUBLIC TRANSPORT**: Castlewellan is served by Ulsterbus 17A, 18, 32 and 518 from points such as Newcastle, Downpatrick, Belfast, Ballynahinch and Banbridge.

## THE WALK

Castlewellan Forest Park covers 460 hectares (1135 acres) and includes substantial areas of deciduous woodland as well as more regimented coniferous plantations. There is an imposing Scottish Baronial-style castle, now used as a Christian conference centre. The Grange Yard, built in 1720 with three courtyards, was once a large farmstead, but now houses an exhibition centre and the Grange Coffee Shop. The Annesley Garden and National Arboretum features formal flowerbeds and a wealth of tree species, and the arrangement ensures that there is always some area showing its best features throughout the changing seasons. With a lake in the centre of the Forest Park, a fine viewpoint at Slievenaslat, and a choice of four colour-coded walking trails, this area offers an impressive amount of interesting walking.

## THE ROUTE

Castlewellan Library is an imposing white building in the Upper Square. There is a large car park and a toilet block alongside, as well as plenty of places offering food and drink. Leave the Upper Square by following the signposted driveway into Castlewellan Forest Park. If you take a car into the forest, there is a small car park beside Castlewellan Lake and a larger car park beside the Grange Yard, with access to the intricate Peace Maze. There is an information board at the lakeside car

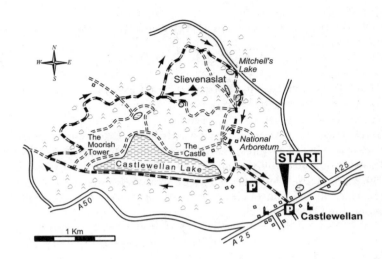

park, showing the layout of the four colour-coded walking trails. There are leaflets available that contain maps of these trails, and it is useful to acquire one from the Ranger's Office before starting this walk.

Walk along the Lake and Sculpture Trail, heading away from the car park by following marker posts bearing yellow arrows. A fine track runs along the southern shore of Castlewellan Lake, which is overhung by a rich variety of trees. As you walk alongside the lake, the castle is seen rising above a sloping lawn on the far side of the water. The sculptures and other features are arranged on the slope to the left. The first is an arrangement of rocks and an earthwork that suggest a megalithic structure. You pass a shelter further along, and there is an old ice house buried under a mound of earth. Next is a standing stone sculpture, followed by two curious wooden pillar sculptures. After passing another shelter, there is a wooden dinosaur whose back is smooth and shiny due to the attention it has received from visiting children!

The lakeside track reaches a junction with other tracks near the head of the lake. Walk straight onwards and uphill on a forest track, looking out for the red arrows marking the course of the Boundary Trail. Avoid a track on the right halfway up the forested slope, but turn right along a narrower path marked by a red arrow at a higher level. The path climbs and drifts to the left before running downhill. When you reach a junction with a broader track, you could make a detour to the right to visit the ruins of the Moorish Tower, a folly which features a view across Castlewellan Lake. The Boundary Trail, however, turns left and climbs further uphill, and a narrow path on the left is signposted for a viewpoint on the edge of the forest. This allows a peep at part of the Mountains of Mourne, as well as to distant Slieve Gullion and nearby Slieve Croob.

Backtrack from the viewpoint and continue along the Boundary Trail, still following red arrows. The path winds downhill and reaches a junction with a broader path. Turn left and follow the path uphill. It runs close to the edge of the forest and features another view of Slieve Croob. The path runs downhill through the forest again, reaching a junction with a gravel track. Walk straight onwards to follow the track uphill. The slope to the right has been cleared and includes a view of the Mountains of Mourne, seen beyond Castlewellan Lake. Climb further

An ornamental fountain in the Annesley Garden.

up the track into taller stands of trees, and turn right along a track marked with a blue arrow to follow the Slievenaslat Trail. There is also a boulder at the junction marked with the direction for Slievenaslat. The track climbs past the Dark Lough, then there is a narrow path on the left marked for Slievenaslat. Follow the path up to an open summit of heather, grass and rock, crowned with a trig point at around 270m (885ft). Views stretch over Castlewellan and Newcastle and across the sea. The Mountains of Mourne visible from here include Slieve Donard, Slieve Commedagh, Slieve Corragh and Slievenaglogh, with Slievelamagan rising beyond. Turning clockwise, the rugged peak of Slieve Bearnagh is followed by the smoother slopes of Slieve Meelmore, Slieve Meelbeg and Slieve Muck. Parts of the Low Mournes and even the Cooley Hills are in view, but the forest trees rise to obscure their more distant profiles. The summit of Slieve Croob can just be seen peeping over the tops of the trees to the north.

Walk back down the path, turn right to follow the broad track past the Dark Lough, and continue downhill to rejoin the red Boundary Trail. Turn right to follow the track uphill from the junction, crossing a rise, then walking downhill. Keep left at a junction of tracks, then right at the next junction, still following red marker arrows. The track passes Mitchell's Lake, which is attractively fringed with reedmace and delightfully mixed woodlands. Cross a stone bridge over the outflowing stream, then turn left along a narrow path marked with red and white arrows. The path passes the Small Duck Pond, then you turn left along the track again. Follow the track uphill to cross another track, then turn left, then right, down a narrower track. Pass a gate at the bottom of the track, and then walk straight though a gateway into the walled Annesley Garden.

The garden has a formal layout with paths running at right angles. The original walled garden dates from 1740 and was 5 hectares (12 acres), but the site was further developed in the 1870s and currently covers an area of 40 hectares (100 acres). The National Arboretum accounts for much of the lower part of the garden, and most of the trees here have their names and country of origin appended. There are small and dainty shrubs, as well as towering sequoias, making an exploration of the area both interesting and highly desirable. As you leave the garden by the main gateway, turn left down a narrow tarmac road. Either bear right to return to the lakeside car park, or walk straight onwards to reach the main car park beyond the Grange Yard, or turn left to follow the driveway back towards Castlewellan.

# WALK 26 – THE WINDY GAP AND LEGANANNY

**START**: At the Windy Gap car park above Gransha – 274431.

**DISTANCE**: 16 kilometres (10 miles).

**TOTAL ASCENT**: 280 metres (920 feet).

**MAPS**: OSNI Discoverer Sheet 20. OSNI Slieve Croob Outdoor Pursuits Map.

**TERRAIN**: Hilly farmland. Several roads, tracks and paths make up the circuit, with some wet and muddy patches.

**DIFFICULTY**: Easy

**PUBLIC TRANSPORT**: Ulsterbus 27 is an infrequent service to Gransha from Dromara and Ballynahinch.

The Legananny Dolmen, a 5000-year-old megalithic monument.

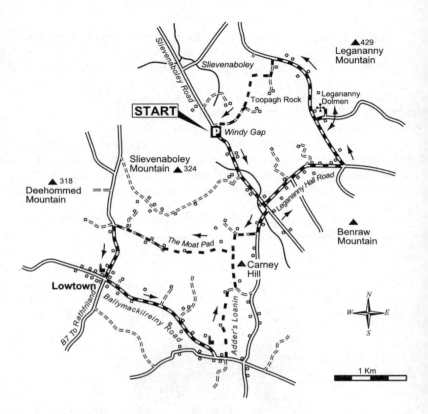

## THE WALK

The Slieve Croob countryside is relatively unknown to most of the walkers who regularly explore the Mountains of Mourne. The low hills surrounding Slieve Croob have an interesting network of rights of way, including both footpaths and bridleways. Some of these rights of way have been cleared, waymarked and signposted by Banbridge District Council, in co-operation with landowners. They bear wonderful names such as the Adder's Loanin and the Moat Pad, and open up a delightful area of countryside between Slieve Croob and the High Mournes. Walkers who take the time to explore the area will find interesting sites such as the Legananny Dolmen, and splendid views of the Mountains of Mourne. The area is largely given over to cattle and sheep grazing, so take care to fasten any gates you use along the way.

## THE ROUTE

There is a car park and viewpoint on top of the Windy Gap, on the Slievenaboley Road above Gransha, near Slieve Croob. Enjoy the extensive view from the car park of the Mountains of Mourne, taking in Slieve Donard, Slieve Commedagh, Slieve Corragh, Slievenaglogh, Cove Mountain, Slievelamagan, Slieve Bearnagh, Slieve Meelmore, Slieve Meelbeg, Slieve Loughshannagh, Carn Mountain, Slieve Muck, Butter Mountain, Cock Mountain and Hen Mountain. By scouting around for a bit more height you can also see the Belfast Hills and Slieve Croob. In really clear weather you would be able to see the distant Sperrin Mountains.

Follow the road downhill from the Windy Gap, in the direction of Leitrim. Pass by the Benraw Orange Hall, which is painted blue, then turn right along Lighthouse Road. The road runs downhill and uphill, then you turn right along a track signposted as the Moat Pad Footpath. Before you reach a house on this track, turn left, right, and left again. The track can be muddy in places and is usually flanked by gorse bushes. Watch for a waymark post showing a right turn through a small gate and up along a narrower track. This track climbs up Carney Hill and enjoys good views southwards to the Mountains of Mourne. Go through a gate at the top of the track, and then walk downhill on a broader grassy track. There is another gate to go through on the way down to a pig farm. Go through one last gate, through the farmyard, and along a concrete road to reach a junction with a tarmac road, then turn left to follow the road down to Lowtown.

There is a shop and bar at Lowtown, where you turn left along the Ballymackilreiny Road. This road undulates through low farmland, passing Derryneil Baptist Church. Turn left at the junction with Millvale Road and pass the derelict Derryneil Orange Hall. On the left is a signpost for the Adder's Loanin Footpath. Cross a wooden step stile beside a gate to follow the fenced, grassy track. Go through a wooden gate and turn left, then right, following the track up past a couple of ruined cottages. Go through a couple of gates to continue uphill. The grassy path runs between hedgerows as it rises through fields, and you go through two small gates on the way. There are fine views back towards the Mountains of Mourne, as well as to the more distant Slieve Foye, the Cooley Hills and Slieve Gullion. Cross a couple of wooden step stiles to pass a farm, then turn right along the concrete farm access road. Turn left up a gravel track that becomes grassy and muddy in places on Carney Hill. When the next farm track is reached, which was followed earlier in the walk, turn right to follow it to the Lighthouse Road. Turn left down the road, then walk uphill and left to the Benraw Orange Hall again.

You could follow the road back up to the car park on the Windy Gap, but there is another loop that can be enjoyed. Turn right at the Benraw Orange Hall and follow Legananny Hall Road uphill. Walk all the way over the highest part of the road, then downhill to a crossroads at the Legananny Orange Hall. Turn left along Legananny Road, which is signposted for the Legananny Dolmen, then follow a few more signposts indicating right and left turns up to the actual dolmen. This is a fine structure, around 5000 years old, with a large tilted triangular capstone perched on three slender stone pillars. There is a fine view from here of the Mountains of Mourne, Slieve Foye, the Cooley Hills and Slieve Gullion.

Retrace your steps down to the Legananny Road and turn right to follow the road onwards. As the road climbs, look out for a footpath sign on the left. Follow the grassy track uphill, but watch for a waymarked right turn up another narrow track. Cross a wooden step stile beside a gate and climb further uphill. Another marker indicates a left turn up a grooved track that is grassy and muddy in places. Cross a step stile beside a gate and continue straight onwards. The track leads down to a road, where a left turn leads straight back to the car park on the Windy Gap. There is one last feature of interest that can be reached on the other side of the road. A short track leads up to a circular hedgerow around a hilltop shrine dedicated to the 'Mother of the Hill'. Flowers and religious artefacts fill the enclosure.

# WALK 27 - SLIEVE CROOB FROM FINNIS

**START**: Finnis (locally known as Massford) – 285477.
**DISTANCE**: 10 kilometres (6 miles).
**TOTAL ASCENT**: 400 metres (1310 feet).
**MAPS**: OSNI Discoverer Sheet 20. OSNI Slieve Croob Outdoor Pursuits Map.
**TERRAIN**: Rugged hillwalking. Minor roads are used on the lower slopes of the hill. The ascent uses a fairly clear track and path, while the descent is along a traffic-free road.
**DIFFICULTY**: Moderate
**PUBLIC TRANSPORT**: Ulsterbus 27 is an infrequent service between Finnis, Dromara and Ballynahinch.

## THE WALK

Slieve Croob is also known as the Twelve Cairns. It is a rugged, isolated little mountain, situated in the northern part of the Mournes AONB. Its position makes it a fine viewpoint not only for the Mountains of Mourne, but also for considerable parts of Ireland and beyond. Almost anyone could climb Slieve Croob, as there is a tarmac road leading practically to the summit, which unfortunately bears an array of communications masts. In the past, people from the surrounding countryside were in the habit of climbing the mountain on the last Sunday in July, known variously as Cairn Sunday, Mountain Sunday or Blaeberry Sunday, and this was an occasion of great festivity. The mountain is also notable for being where the River Lagan rises, gathering strength in the Slieve Croob countryside to become a fine river by the time it reaches the city of Belfast.

## THE ROUTE

Start in the little village of Finnis, locally known as Massford, which lies on the northern slopes of Slieve Croob near Dromara and Ballynahinch. There is no car park in the village, but you can park beside the road in front of a housing development called Massford Close. King's Pub, near a bridge spanning the River Lagan, is reputed to be the smallest, oldest and most haunted pub in Ireland. A spirit exorcised from the pub lived in a blasted tree nearby, only

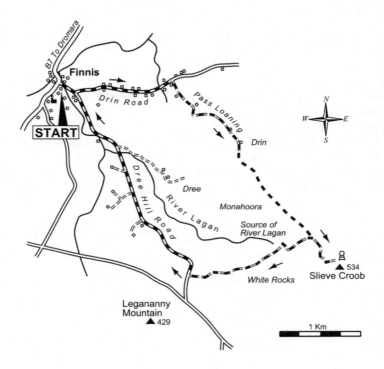

recently removed. Peter Morgan's Cottage, a pre-Famine house near the bridge, was recently restored.

Follow the Dree Hill Road up out of Finnis for a short way, and turn left along the Drin Road. This road rises and falls and has a number of houses along its length. There are good views over the lowland countryside to the left. Watch out for a traditional whitewashed house on the left of the road. On the right, directly opposite the house, is a concrete lane known as the Pass Loaning. Walk up the lane, passing a few farm outbuildings and a well. Although there are high banks on either side of the lane, there is a view ahead to a small plantation of conifers and the mountain slopes beyond. The lane bends to the right and is flanked by dry stone walls, climbing gently uphill as its concrete surface changes to a stony surface. Climb past two old houses, now unoccupied, and continue through a metal gate onto the more open mountain slopes. As the track climbs, it is flanked by the tumbled remains of dry stone walls that once enclosed it, and the line of the path leading onwards becomes more difficult to trace. It runs along as a rugged groove and it is actually easier to walk alongside it. The grassy slope on this part of the mountain is known as Monahoora, and this is a good place to listen for skylarks or spot buzzards. If you drift to the left as you climb, there are fences that lead onwards and upwards. Cross these at the ladder stiles provided, and follow a faint path to the left that drifts towards another gate and stile. There is some boggy ground to cross before you reach a tarmac road beyond. Simply turn left and follow the road to the top of Slieve Croob.

There is an array of communication masts enclosed by fences on the mountain, but to reach the true summit you should follow a fence steeply uphill alongside the edge of the second enclosure and cross another fence using a step stile. The remains of what was once a large summit cairn stands beside a trig point at 534m (1755ft). Views from this point are naturally very extensive as the slopes fall away to low ground on all sides. The Mountains of Mourne are displayed as a line of rounded humps to the south, followed by the distant Slieve Foye, the Cooley Hills and Slieve Gullion. On a clear day you can see beyond Lough Neagh to the Sperrin Mountains and northwards to the Belfast Hills. The Galloway coast of Scotland and the Isle of Man may also be seen over the sea.

Return to the road and follow it downhill in sweeping zigzags from the communications masts. Look out for the source of the River Lagan, which is a mere trickle where it flows down from the road – it is hard to imagine that it becomes a great river, flowing through the city of Belfast. The road later runs more gently down to a gateway and car park on the Dree Hill Road. It is possible for almost anyone to park here and follow the road up onto Slieve Croob, but maybe that is too easy for most walkers! Turn right to follow the Dree Hill Road gently downhill, then a little more steeply. There are views along the valley of the infant River Lagan, and the road crosses the river at the foot of the slope. Simply continue along the road, which runs roughly parallel to the river, to return to the village of Finnis.

The buzzard, a large hawklike bird
of prey, soars through the air
in wide circles.

# WALK 28 – THE MOURNE WALL WALK

**START**: Silent Valley car park – 306209.

**DISTANCE**: 32 kilometres (20 miles).

**TOTAL ASCENT**: 2800 metres (9185 feet).

**MAPS**: OSNI Discoverer Sheet 29. OSNI Mourne Country Outdoor Pursuits Map. Harvey's Mourne Mountains.

**TERRAIN**: Mountainous. There are some very steep and rocky slopes on this tough walk, along with some wet and boggy patches. The Mourne Wall is generally easy to follow even in mist and poor visibility, but there are some moves away from it. Keep a careful check on progress and on the weather as you go, and be sure to take note of escape routes in case of fatigue or the onset of poor weather.

**DIFFICULTY**: Difficult

**PUBLIC TRANSPORT**: Ulsterbus 405 is a summer-only service around the Mountains of Mourne, running past the Silent Valley. If you descend from the route early, it is useful to know of other Ulsterbus services on the roads below.

## THE WALK

The Mourne Wall Walk is surely one of the greatest mountain walks in Ireland. Between 1957 and 1984 a walk around the wall was organised on an annual basis by the Youth Hostels Association of Northern Ireland. As the numbers increased, so did erosion on the ground close to the wall, and amid growing concerns the event was cancelled. The walk was surely the largest mass participation event ever held in the mountains, attracting some 4000 people on a single day, and there has never been anything like it since. Although the mass event no longer takes place, there are still individuals and small groups of walkers who set out to walk around the course of the Mourne Wall. The route can be conveniently covered starting from the Silent Valley, which is the lowest point on the wall and a popular visitor attraction. If you intend taking a car into the valley, please be aware of the limited opening times on the gate, usually 10am to 6pm. It might be better to arrange for a car to drop you off and meet you later on the public road near Colligan Bridge. The course of the Mourne Wall on either side of the Silent Valley is disappointing, and in places it seems to be a haphazard

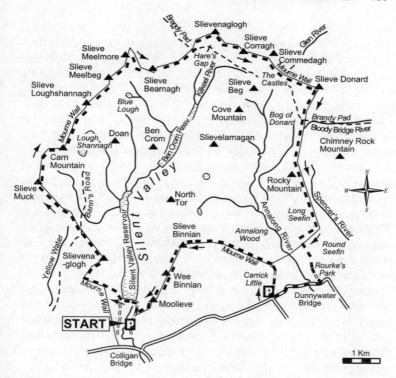

construction. The truly 'classic' proportions of the wall are found northwards of Carn Mountain and Long Seefin, and there are some particularly stout sections on Slieve Corragh and the Bog of Donard. Monumental stone lookout towers appear on Slieve Meelmore, Slieve Commedagh and Slieve Donard. Before you attempt this walk, take a serious look at the statistics and at the map, and ask yourself if you are really fit enough to attempt it in a day!

## THE ROUTE

If you arrive at the Silent Valley with a car, bear in mind that you may not be able to enter until 10am, and you will have to remove your car by 6pm. It is possible for walkers to enter and leave the valley earlier and later. From the main gates, simply follow the road straight through the mixed woodlands to reach the Silent Valley Reservoir dam. Turn left and walk across the top of the dam to reach a shelter on the far side. Turn right along a track and follow a broad gravel path winding uphill. Watch carefully for a vague path off to the right at a bend, leading up a slope of gorse, heather and tussocky grass. When you reach a fence, cross it using a wooden step stile and turn left to follow it uphill. A wall rises further up the slope, and you will have a view of a broad and boggy hollow. The Mourne Wall at this stage avoids the bog by climbing further uphill before turning sharply right to approach Slievenaglogh. The slopes of this first mountain are steep and littered with angular blocks and boulders, needing great care all the way to the top. No point in exhausting yourself at this early stage! The wall reaches the heathery summit of the mountain at 445m (1450ft) and there is a chance to gaze round at some of the higher mountains to be crossed during this epic walk.

Cross the wall using a ladder stile and follow it downhill. The slope is steep, with rock and heather giving way to some boggy patches. There is a broad gap to cross, and you will pass a stout iron gate with a ladder stile beside it. Don't cross the wall, but stay on the same side, where you can walk along a stony track running roughly parallel to the wall. This should offer a better surface underfoot than the surrounding heather. The track drifts away from the Mourne Wall and passes through a gap in another wall. Drift back towards the Mourne Wall and follow it up the steep, heathery slopes of Slieve Muck. While this section of the Mourne Wall may not assume the classic proportions found on other parts, it is still a faultless guide to the summit. There are a couple of steep stretches where the wall was never built, and lengths of tangled wire fencing fill the gaps. Granite slabs cause the first gap. The second gap is on a crumbled outcrop of older mudstone. The grassy summit of Slieve Muck rises to a trig point at an altitude of 673m (2198ft) and is splendidly situated to offer good views of the High and Low Mournes.

Cross a ladder stile at a junction of walls, so that you can follow the course of the Mourne Wall roughly northwards to descend from the summit. There are outcrops of rock along the way, and then the sudden appearance of a small cliff causes a diversion away to the right. Follow the wall across a gap, then a grassy strip beside the wall leads up onto the heathery summit of Carn Mountain at 588m (1919ft). There is a junction of walls at this point, and the Mourne Wall suddenly assumes its 'classic' proportions and becomes a much more substantial structure than the wall that has been followed so far. Follow the wall downhill and over a subsidiary hump, then down to a gap.

There is a strip of short grass beside the wall, with heather and bilberry stretching away from it. The wall leads to the summit of Slieve

Loughshannagh at 620m (2030ft), where there are low rounded boulders of granite and a small cairn. Walk steeply down to the next gap on the grassy strip close to the wall, with more rugged grass and heather slopes further away. The wall next leads steeply uphill, still with a grassy strip close by, and heather and small boulders further away. The gradient eases towards the top, where the Mourne Wall turns right. There is a cairn on the other side of the wall marking the summit of Slieve Meelbeg at 708m (2310ft).

Looking ahead, you can see the stone lookout tower on Slieve Meelmore. Slieve Commedagh is smooth slopes are seen rising beyond Slieve Bearnagh's rocky tors. Slieve Donard is also in view, as well as the knobbly crest of Slieve Binnian and the little hump of Wee Binnian. All these mountains have to be crossed in due course on this monstrous roller-coaster route.

Follow the wall down a steep slope of short grass embedded with small boulders. Pass a ladder stile on the gap, and then let the wall lead you up a stony slope onto Slieve Meelmore. The wall crosses a heathery shoulder, then climbs up another stony slope. Notice how the Mourne Wall slices through the course of an older stone wall. Follow the wall along the crest, crossing the highest part of the mountain. There is a stout granite lookout tower, built in 1921, tucked into a sharp corner in the wall at 680m (2237ft). Some maps wrongly credit this point with a much greater height.

A steep and stony slope, littered with angular boulders and some rock steps, leads down to a deeply-cut gap, where there is a ladder stile over the Mourne Wall. Do not cross it, but climb steeply up the rocky slopes of Slieve Bearnagh. The path drifts away from the wall, and the wall itself features a gap where its builders were defeated by a steep, slabby rockface. Continue steeply uphill on a bouldery slope beside the wall. At the top, you will realise that the highest part of Slieve Bearnagh is off to the right, where a large granite tor thrusts skywards from a gentle shoulder of short grass. If you wish to climb all the way to the top, you will need to use your hands to scramble over the blocky outcrops, making this one of the toughest Mourne summits to bring underfoot. The altitude is 739m (2394ft). There is a fine view back towards the Silent Valley Reservoir.

The path drifts away from the Mourne Wall to descend from Slieve Bearnagh. A couple of other granite tors cause breaks in the wall, so anyone following its exact course must be prepared for more hands-on scrambling. The path drops steeply on a grassy slope that becomes

Walking on the Mourne Wall on the slopes of Slieve Donard.

bouldery. A heathery shoulder bears a few rocky outcrops, then the wall drops steeply downhill again. Beware of a break in the wall, where there is another short, slabby cliff face. Keep well to the right to find a flight of stone steps leading down to a cairn built around a metal post on the Hare's Gap.

In case of fatigue or the onset of poor weather, it is possible to head from the Hare's Gap straight down to the Ben Crom Reservoir and so return directly to the Silent Valley Reservoir. Alternatively, the course of the Brandy Pad slices across the mountainsides, offering a route that is well away from the course of the Mourne Wall, but also offering rapid onward progress if needed.

Leaving the Hare's Gap, climb up a flight of granite steps, where a steep and slabby rock face causes a gap in the course of the Mourne Wall. When the wall resumes its course, it is of truly monumental proportions, as there was never any shortage of building material alongside on this stretch. You can clearly discern 'plug and feather' marks in the blocks where they were split. There are huge 'footing' stones, several projecting 'through' stones in the middle of the wall, and well-laid 'cam' stones on top of the wall. Walk past a ladder stile on a shoulder of Slievenaglogh, and then continue gently uphill, walking on short grass or granite slabs close to the wall, with heather and boulders alongside. A large cairn marks the summit, sitting on a granite platform to the right at 586m (1922ft). The name 'Diamond Rocks' on maps refers to a particularly crystalline outcrop of granite.

Continue downhill, following the Mourne Wall across a slight gap, then climb over a subsidiary summit before following the wall down to a slightly lower gap. Climb steadily uphill on the slopes of Slieve Corragh. The summit features low and rounded outcrops of granite at around 640m (2100ft). The wall turns left and runs downhill a short way, following a steep-sided crest as it crosses another gap. This is one of the narrowest ridges in the Mountains of Mourne, but it isn't really apparent as the wall prevents you from seeing both sides of the ridge at the same time. A steep grassy slope needs to be climbed next, and there is a pipe dispensing clear spring water if you need to quench your thirst on the ascent. As the gradient eases you reach a prominent stone lookout tower whose doorway lintel is carved with the date 1913. This is not quite on the summit of Slieve Commedagh, but is perched on a shoulder offering excellent views. The true summit of Slieve Commedagh lies across the wall, at an altitude of 767m (2512ft).

Follow the wall downhill. A steep, grassy slope gives way to a level shoulder, then another steep grassy slope leads down to a broad gap, with Slieve Donard looming ahead. There is a double stone step stile over the wall, but you don't need to cross it; simply climb straight uphill. The slope is steep and grassy, with small embedded boulders in places. The gradient is unremitting and it is not possible to see the summit until almost there. A prominent lookout tower, dated 1910, sits cosily in a corner of the Mourne Wall, providing a shelter that is only marginally better than being out in the rain. A trig point is mounted on top of the tower, at an altitude of 850m (2796ft). There is a large cairn on the other side of the wall, called the Great Carn. It may contain stones from St Domangard's fifth-century mountain-top oratory.

Views from the summit of Slieve Donard are remarkably extensive, and in clear weather can extend far beyond the Mountains of Mourne to the Wicklow Mountains beyond Dublin, to County Antrim and the Galloway Hills of Scotland, and out to sea to the Isle of Man. A more usual view would comprise the following features: To the south, neighbouring Chimney Rock Mountain and Rocky Mountain give way to the farmlands of the Kingdom of Mourne and the mouth of

Carlingford Lough. Turning clockwise, Slieve Binnian's rugged crest gives way to a distant view of Slieve Foye and Slieve Martin, before the North Tor rises closer to hand. Beyond Slievelamagan, the Cooley Hills, Eagle Mountain and Slieve Muck can be seen. Cove Mountain and Doan lead the eye to Carn Mountain and distant Slieve Gullion. After nearby Slieve Beg come Slieve Loughshannagh, Slieve Meelbeg, rugged Slieve Bearnagh, Slieve Meelmore and the Hare's Gap. Slieve Commedagh is close to Slieve Donard, but there are also distant views of Slieve Croob, Dundrum Bay and St John's Point.

Follow the Mourne Wall steeply down the southern slopes of Slieve Donard, on the same side as the Annalong Valley. The slope is steep and grassy, with a few rashes of embedded boulders. Rugged heather slopes close in on the wall before it levels out on the Bog of Donard. Crossing the Bog of Donard, the ground near the wall is nearly always wet and boggy, but it becomes drier as the wall runs further southwards. Some walkers prefer to walk on top of the wall to keep their feet dry, but there is a narrow, stony path through the rugged heather beside the wall later, crossing a shallow dip in the moorland. The wall turns slightly to the left, slicing across the slopes of Rocky Mountain and passing a partially filled gap where there was once a gateway. You begin to get the feeling that the wall is deliberately avoiding the summits. Follow the wall along a heathery shoulder to Long Seefin. There is a stony, gritty path alongside. Alternatively, you can follow a path which drifts away from the wall southwards down the slope, though it does get rather bouldery later. The Mourne Wall on Long Seefin reaches a curious little tower at a corner, and the construction of the wall ceases to display the 'classic' proportions seen on the higher mountains. The remaining lengths of the wall on this walk are less substantial structures. Follow the wall straight down a rugged slope, alongside a forest, to reach an iron gate leading onto a walled track. Some walkers follow the Mourne Wall straight across the Annalong River, but you should really use the tracks and roads described below to reach the wall's continuation on the far side of the valley.

Turn left to follow the track through a small part of the forest, going through another gate to leave the forest. Keep straight on along the track, with the forest to the left and gorse bushes to the right. The track, known as the Dunnywater Track, is grass and bare granite, but later it is surfaced with gravel as it passes farms and houses. When you reach the road below, turn right to follow it. There is a prominent waterworks gateway, featuring four pinnacled towers. Continuing along the road, cross the Dunnywater Bridge, and climb uphill to reach the Carrick Little car park. If you've had enough at this point, then the car park is a handy place to arrange to be collected. Slieve Binnian still remains as a formidable obstacle to the successful completion of the walk.

An obvious gravel track flanked by gorse bushes rises beside the car park. The gentle ascent leads past a couple of buildings and the bouldery field walls alongside become quite substantial. Cross a stone step stile beside an iron gate. The Mourne Wall rises to the left, offering a direct line to the summit of Slieve Binnian. There is a grassy strip alongside the wall, with more rugged slopes of heather and boulders further away. As the wall approaches the huge granite summit tor on Slieve Binnian, you will realise that the wall was never constructed all the way over the top. Drift to the right to pass through a gap in the tor. If you wish to climb all the way to the summit at 747m (2449ft), you will have to grapple with the rock. A length of wire fencing was stretched over the summit, but all that remains are a few bent iron posts and tangles of rusting wire. Do not attempt to follow the line of this old fence, which quickly leads onto dangerously greasy slabs.

Pass through the gap in the summit tor to start the descent towards the Silent Valley. Keep well away from the slabs of granite, and also take care on the rough and bouldery slopes that fall steeply below them. Inch back towards the course of the Mourne Wall, and cross to the other side when you reach a convenient gap. The bouldery slope eventually gives way to a gentler grassy gap between Slieve Binnian and Wee Binnian. Although the wall climbs straight up Wee Binnian, there are unseen cliffs on the far side and it is better to head to the left and pass through a notch on the shoulder of the hill. A deeply eroded path runs down the far side, then an easier strip of grass leads further downhill.

Go through an iron gate to walk on the other side of the wall, climbing gently up the side of Moolieve. There are piles of stony rubble on the summit, then you walk fairly close to the wall on a grassy strip with heather closing in on the foot of the wall. The path beside the wall eventually vanishes as a junction is reached with a fence. You will need to step across the fence and walk through some low, prickly gorse scrub to reach a gravel path and the Silent Valley road below. The last few paces of this walk are particularly uncomfortable! Once the road is reached, simply turn left to walk either back to the car park or out of the main gates of the Silent Valley.

# WALK 29 - ULSTER WAY - NEWRY TO ROSTREVOR

**START**: Newry Town Hall – 086267.
**FINISH**: The Square in Rostrevor – 179184.
**DISTANCE**: 18 kilometres (11 miles).
**TOTAL ASCENT**: 360 metres (1180 feet).
**MAPS**: OSNI Discoverer Sheet 29. OSNI Mourne Country Outdoor Pursuits Map and Harvey Mourne Mountains cover only the final part of the route.
**TERRAIN**: Almost all along hilly minor roads, though there is a short stretch through fields that can be muddy.
**DIFFICULTY**: Easy
**PUBLIC TRANSPORT**: Newry has a railway station, linking with Belfast and Dublin. There are also Ulsterbus and Bus Éireann services linking Newry with Belfast and Dublin. Ulsterbus 39 links Newry with Rostrevor. Ulsterbus 39F is a very occasional service through Burren.

## THE WALK

Earlier editions of this book contained a four-day route called the 'Mourne Trail', which was part of the Ulster Way. Parts have been re-named as the Mourne Way and Lecale Way. The original course of the Ulster Way is followed out of the bustling city of Newry and climbs into low hilly countryside. The rollercoaster route passes close to the village of Burren on its way to Rostrevor, and there are tantalising glimpses towards the Mountains of Mourne along the way. You could walk this stretch easily enough without any special gear, travelling light and relying on the regular bus services between Newry and Rostrevor later in the day. It is interesting to watch how the Mountains of Mourne gradually take shape beyond Newry, with fertile farmland giving way to more rugged little hills. If you need accommodation, there are plenty of places to stay in Newry, which was granted city status in 2002, and quite a few around Rostrevor.

## THE ROUTE

Newry Town Hall is an obvious starting point and a walk along Hill Street offers an interesting way through town, though you can also leave town via The Mall, which runs beside the Clanrye River. Hill Street is the

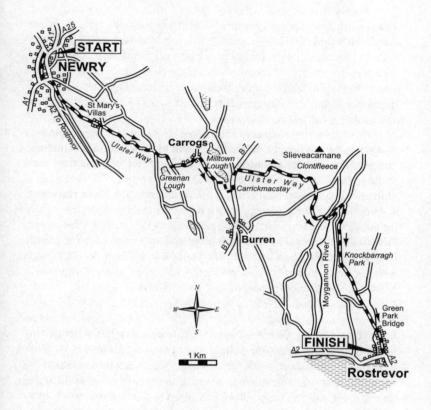

town's main shopping street and most of it is pedestrianised. It has two squares, Margaret Square and Marcus Square, after which you reach the imposing granite Cathedral of St Patrick and St Colman. It dates from 1829 and was the first Roman Catholic cathedral to be built in Ireland after the Emancipation, when civil and religious freedoms were restored to Catholics. The interior is especially ornate. Further along the street is St Mary's Church of Ireland, which was begun in 1810 as a replacement for the older St Patrick's, whose tower can be seen rising above town. The tiny St Colman's Park is opposite. At the end of Hill Street is the First Presbyterian Church, dating from 1853. Newry has a wealth of history spread through its streets. The character of the town used to be proclaimed in the rhyme: 'High church, low steeple, dirty streets and proud people.'

Turn left at the end of Hill Street and walk up a busy main road. Use a subway to cross to the other side, then walk through the Abbey Yard. Although no trace remains, a Cistercian abbey was built in this area by St Malachy in the twelfth century. According to tradition, however, Newry was founded when St Patrick planted a yew tree at the head of Carlingford Lough. Walk along Boat Street, passing the Schooner Lounge, both reminders that this part of town was once the quayside for the old port of Newry.

Start climbing in earnest up Chapel Street, passing a Roman Catholic chapel dated 1790. The road climbs past a recycling centre and the gradient eases at a staggered crossroads near a row of houses called St Mary's Villas. The road continues on a gently undulating course through fields, passing scattered houses, then drops down through a crossroads to follow Lower Carrogs Road. A pig farm sits in the bottom of the valley, and from here there is a view of the crest of Slieve Foye. The road bends right and left as it climbs, with a view across the reedy Greenan Lough. Note that the road is marked as 'Corrags Road' as it climbs, which is surely a misspelling. After it rolls past a few houses at Carrogs, a right turn is marked as Carrogs Road.

A track on the left leads down towards a farm overlooking the little pool of Milltown Lough, but don't follow it. Instead, continue further down Carrogs Road and take the next farm track on the left. After passing through the farmyard, turn right along an old track bounded by trees, crossing ground which can be muddy when wet. A left turn later leads up to another road, the B7, where a left turn is made uphill. It is worth noting at this point that the little village of Burren is just to the south. It has a heritage centre, as well as a cottage where Jim Larkin, fiery leader of the Irish labour movement in the early twentieth century, spent his boyhood.

Keep to the right at a fork when following the B7 road uphill, passing the Care Trade building. Take the next road to the right, which climbs uphill past a few buildings, then bends left and right before crossing the hill. The highest part of the road runs at nearly 230m (750ft), on the shoulder of Craignamona. Your view as you walk extends from Slieve Martin to Slieve Foye, though the Cooley Hills to Slieve Gullion and Camlough Mountain. Follow the road down past a farm and on through a crossroads on the valley side. Continue along the road, which drops down past Clontifleece National School, where a plaque records that it was 'Erected by Narcissus Batt Esq. 1839'. Turn quickly right and left down Lurgancanty Road onto another road and cross over the Moygannon River.

Follow the road uphill, turning right at the second junction, which is the Upper Knockbarragh Road. The road climbs past a small covered reservoir and descends past a few farms. There are good views across to the Cooley Hills and you may notice the large derelict house called Knockbarragh Park on the right. After passing a belt of oak, beech and sycamore trees, you can see down to Rostrevor on the shores of Carlingford Lough. The road runs down past a huddle of houses at Drumreagh Park and crosses Park Bridge. Continue past a

Our Lady Star of the Sea Roman Catholic church in Rostrevor.

Gaelic football ground and pass by the houses at St Rita's Park. At the end of Greenpark Road, turn left to reach The Square in the middle of Rostrevor. Many of the buildings sport a colourful lick of paint, while there is seating and car parking under a handful of fine oak trees. The broad Church Street narrows as it runs beside the Church of Ireland and continues uphill to the Roman Catholic church, but the Ulster Way continues to the right along Bridge Street. For the time being, there are a handful of shops and pubs, places to eat and places to stay. The nearby Kilbroney Park provides a campsite.

Kilbroney's name is derived from St Bronagh's Church, though this is off the course of the Ulster Way. The ruins of the sixth-century church remain, surrounded by an ancient graveyard. An artefact known as St Bronagh's Bell resides in an alcove in the Roman Catholic church. It is said that the bell used to hang in a tree, then was forgotten about until the tree was felled and the bell was rediscovered. It is over a thousand years old, and you can hear its sound by striking it with a rubber mallet!

# WALK 30 - MOURNE WAY - ROSTREVOR TO OTT TRACK

**START**: The Square in Rostrevor – 179184.
**FINISH**: Ott Track car park – 280277.
**DISTANCE**: 20 kilometres (12½ miles).
**TOTAL ASCENT**: 880 metres (2890 feet).
**MAPS**: OSNI Discoverer Sheet 29. OSNI Mourne Country Outdoor Pursuits Map.
**TERRAIN**: Forested and mountainous. The route follows a series of forest tracks, then switches to rugged mountains where the ground can be boggy and heathery, or steep and rocky.
**DIFFICULTY**: Moderate
**PUBLIC TRANSPORT**: Ulsterbus 39 links Rostrevor with Newry. Ulsterbus 405 is a summer service from Newcastle, passing the Ott Track car park.

## THE WALK

The Mourne Trail leaves Rostrevor and passes through Kilbroney Park to reach Rostrevor Forest. A series of forest tracks and paths are linked to rise gradually through the forest and out onto a more open gap sparsely planted with Scots pine. As it approaches Leitrim Lodge, the route climbs into a valley and then crosses gaps in the mountains before scaling Slievemoughanmore and Pigeon Rock Mountain. These two summits are the highest points gained on the Mourne Trail, and indeed on the whole of the Ulster Way. The waymarking is mainly in the form of wooden posts. In Rostrevor Forest these bear a yellow arrow, while over the mountains they are more widely spaced and bear an orange arrow and a 'walking man' symbol. This section of the route ends on the Deer's Meadow, but you should bear in mind that this is some distance from any accommodation, and there is only an infrequent summer bus service along the road. It might be best to arrange to be collected from the route at the end of the day. The nearest bed and breakfast is a house called Hillview at Attical.

## THE ROUTE

Leave Rostrevor by following Bridge Street, crossing the river at the entrance to the Fairy Glen. While the Mourne Way technically runs

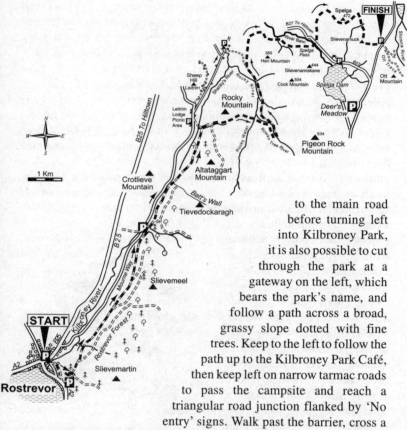

to the main road before turning left into Kilbroney Park, it is also possible to cut through the park at a gateway on the left, which bears the park's name, and follow a path across a broad, grassy slope dotted with fine trees. Keep to the left to follow the path up to the Kilbroney Park Café, then keep left on narrow tarmac roads to pass the campsite and reach a triangular road junction flanked by 'No entry' signs. Walk past the barrier, cross a river and follow the tarmac road into Rostrevor Forest.

When the road turns left to leave the forest, turn right along a track, which climbs rather steeply uphill. As the gradient eases, there are two stretches of track running along the edge of the forest overlooking the fields. Keep straight on at a track junction, crossing the slope on an undulating course, but generally heading uphill. Keep going straight at another junction where there are good views across the valley over the tops of young trees. Go through two barrier gates and continue along the track, passing a Water Service building. Continue on the track, turning left down a gravel path to reach a footbridge where the Yellow Water River pours down a waterfall. Cross over the footbridge and then turn quickly left and right along tracks.

There has been some clear felling and replanting around the head of the valley. Cross a stile beside a gate at the edge of the forest, then drift right to follow a path that can be muddy, running up and down across a bracken slope which is sparsely wooded. Cross a stream and turn up a path which takes you round a stand of forest. Look out for a Mass Rock on the right, in the form of a large boulder of granite at Altataggart. When many Catholic practices were banned under the Penal Laws of the eighteenth century, Mass was often held in remote places using a suitable stone as an altar. Follow the track onwards as it runs across another thinly wooded slope and note how many fine Scots pines grow here. A grassy, stony path cuts through the bracken and begins to descend. Walk through a gate in the wall and cross a river at a ford made of granite slabs. Turn right up a track, and when it bends right across the hillside, leave it and climb straight uphill beside a little stream. A clear path leads to a gap between Tornamrock and Rocky Mountain, at 325m (1065ft). Walk straight down the other side and cross Rocky Water, then turn right and follow Rowan Tree River upstream. Looking across the stream, a clear track can be seen. At some point the river needs to be crossed, but it isn't clearly marked. If the river is low and there are plenty of boulder stepping stones, then short-cut straight across. Follow the track on the other side downstream and it soon pulls away from the river.

The majestic Scots pine.

The track runs across the foot of Hen Mountain and is clearly heading towards low-lying fields and a road, where there is a car park near the Rocky River Bridge. However, before reaching a gate and passing between the fields, turn right to leave the track and stay on the open moorland slopes of Hen Mountain. A path follows the field boundaries for a while, then drifts to the right into a boggy hollow beside the infant River Bann, around 165m (540ft).

Watch for a path climbing gently from the river, and later swing left over the rugged lower slopes of Slievenamiskan. Drop back towards the River Bann and cross it at a footbridge. Walk up to a small enclosure and go through two gates to reach the B27 road on the Spelga Pass, far below the Spelga Dam. There is no bus service on this road, and as there is no car park closer than the dam, a pick-up could be awkward to arrange.

Cross the road and cross a ladder stile beside a nearby gate. A path follows a fence and a wall uphill and around the rugged slopes of Spelga. As soon as a little stream crosses the path, turn right and follow it uphill. Link with a bendy path above 450m (1475ft) and follow it over the higher parts of Spaltha. Watch carefully for a right turn, following another path across a valley where there are old turf cuttings. As the path rises, turn left to pass the summit of Slievenamuck, at 504m (1654ft).

Drop downhill, pass beneath a power line, cross a ladder stile and reach a road at a small car park near the start of the Ott Track. Either arrange to be collected here, or in the summer months, turn up in time to catch the Mourne Rambler bus service.

# WALK 31 - MOURNE WAY - OTT TRACK TO NEWCASTLE

**START**: Ott Track car park – 280277.
**FINISH**: The Youth Hostel in Newcastle – 379314.
**DISTANCE**: 20 kilometres (12½ miles).
**TOTAL ASCENT**: 170 metres (560 feet).
**MAPS**: OSNI Discoverer Sheet 29. OSNI Mourne Country Outdoor Pursuits Map.
**TERRAIN**: Low hills, forest and farmland. The route follows roads, tracks and paths for the most part, but some stretches can be boggy and wet.
**DIFFICULTY**: Moderate
**PUBLIC TRANSPORT**: Ulsterbus 405 is a summer service from Newcastle, passing the Ott Track car park. Several Ulsterbus services converge on Newcastle, including 17, 17A, 18, 20, 26B, 32, 34, 34B, 36 and 37.

The stony Trassey Track beside Clonachullion Wood.

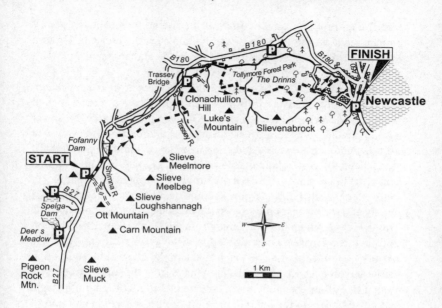

## THE WALK

The Mourne Way leaves the Ott Track car park and follows the road down towards the Fofanny Dam. A boggy hillside and the Trassey Track give way to farm tracks and forest tracks around Tollymore. The Mourne Way runs alongside the Shimna River, climbs high on the southern side of the Tollymore Forest Park, then descends through farmland to approach Newcastle. The route threads its way through Newcastle's suburbs and passes through Castle Park to reach the sea and a promenade path. Waymarking on this stretch includes metal Mourne Way signposts beside the roads and a variety of wooden marker posts for this and other trails in the Tollymore Forest Park. There is plenty of accommodation in and around Newcastle, including hotels, guesthouses, bed and breakfasts, a youth hostel and campsites.

## THE ROUTE

Start at the car park near the Ott Track and simply walk down the Slievenamon Road, overlooking the River Shimna. Continue down the road until a small forest is reached on the right. A ladder stile beside a gate gives access to a slope that can be followed down alongside the forest. Cut through a small corner of the forest, then follow a grassy embankment on the far side of the Fofanny Dam Reservoir. Cross a little footbridge over a channel at the end of the embankment, but don't cross the dam.

Cross a ladder stile to discover a track leading away from the dam, and follow it around the hillside. Turn right along a narrower path marked by occasional concrete posts. The path in fact marks the line of a water pipeline, which is exposed from time to time along the way. Cut off down into a little valley and cross a stream, climbing up a flight of stone steps to cross a ladder stile at the top. A path can be followed across the lower slopes of Slieve Meelmore, running roughly parallel to a dry stone wall, but generally keeping well above it. The slope is mostly grassy, but has some stony patches along the way. Cross over the Trassey River, which tumbles down from the Hare's Gap, then turn left to follow the Trassey Track through a gateway. A path known as the Brandy Pad runs this way, along which smugglers once brought illicit spirits and other goods across the mountains from the small harbours on the coast. Follow the stony track onwards, with the forest to the right and gorse bushes to the left. Go through another gate and enter part of Clonachullion Wood. At a final gate, cross a stone step stile beside the gate to reach a minor road. Turn right to walk a short way down the road, then turn right again to pass above a car park.

A gravel track leads to a junction of three tracks. Take the middle one, then cross three stiles beside three gates on the way to Tollymore Forest Park. A gentle rise on the track passes the Salmon Leap viewpoint, then there is a slight descent to cross Maria's Bridge, where there is a waterfall off to the right. Walk downstream to cross the Boundary Bridge and continue downstream to cross Parnell's Bridge. Walk further downstream, but don't cross the Rustic Bridge or Altavaddy Bridge. The route turns right to climb through forest beside the Spinkwee River. Pass the Cascade Falls and Spinkwee Bridge, later turning left to cross Hore's Bridge, which bears a datemark of 1824.

After crossing Hore's Bridge, keep straight on along a broad track. A narrow, muddy path is followed uphill to the right, cutting out a bend in the track. Turn right, then left, then rise gradually alongside the inside edge of the forest again. Turn right at a junction of tracks where a rock is inscribed with the words 'To the Mountain Top 1826' with a red hand giving the direction. If you choose to go that way, note that the height of the trees cuts out any chance of a view! The forest track descends gently at first, with a view across a rugged mountain gap to the right, and later zigzags, allowing you to take in fine views over Newcastle, Murlough, St John's Point and St Patrick's Country. Take the track to the right at a junction, zigzagging down to some gates. Go straight through, then continue down a narrow tarmac road, passing a few houses.

When a junction is reached at a bend, keep walking downhill a short way, then turn left along a gravelly lane signposted as a public footpath. This is Tipperary Lane, leading down past a handful of houses, the last one being the large Tipperary House. Follow the Shimna River downstream and note the fine mixture of tree species along the way in Tipperary Wood, as well as gorse, broom and bracken. Turn left and cross a road bridge over the Shimna River, then turn right to follow a tarmac path further downstream, passing manicured grassy areas and benches. Cross a broad footbridge and let the path lead you to another footbridge over another river, then cross the busy Bryansford Road. Walk past the play areas and boating pool in Castle Park, then join a busy road in Newcastle. The Tourist Information Centre is off to the right. Newcastle's main shopping street is off to the left.

Cross over the road, turning left to cross the bridge over the Shimna River, then follow the road path along the promenade. Towards the end of the promenade you will see the funnel-shaped Roman Catholic church and the Slieve Donard Hotel; the youth hostel is located between the two. This side of Newcastle is essentially a seaside resort, with a full range of accommodation options, as well as plenty of shops, pubs and restaurants. It is quite separate from the older harbour area on the southern side of town. The huge dome of Slieve Donard, rising to 850m (2796ft), completely dominates the town. An ascent, which on a fine day might well be the crowning glory of a walk along the Mourne Way, is an optional extra you might like to consider (see Walk 21).

# WALK 32 – LECALE WAY – NEWCASTLE TO CLOUGH

**START**: The Youth Hostel in Newcastle – 379314.
**FINISH**: At the castle in Clough village – 409403.
**DISTANCE**: 13 kilometres (8 miles).
**TOTAL ASCENT**: 65 metres (215 feet).
**MAPS**: OSNI Discoverer Sheets 21 and 29. OSNI Mourne Country Outdoor Pursuits Map covers only the first part of the route.
**TERRAIN**: Coastal. The route follows the beach, as well as roads, tracks and paths near the shore. Very high tides could be a problem at the start, so be sure to consult local tide tables before starting.
**DIFFICULTY**: Easy
**PUBLIC TRANSPORT**: Several Ulsterbus services converge on Newcastle, including 17, 17A, 18, 20, 26B, 32, 34, 34B, 36 and 37. Ulsterbus 17, 17A and 20 link Newcastle, Dundrum and Clough.

## THE WALK

This section of the Lecale Way is essentially a coastal route from Newcastle to Dundrum and Clough. The initial stages are along the beach, so that you can walk along a broad expanse of sand when the tide is out, but a high tide will press you onto a higher storm beach and may actually prevent your walk for a while. There are a number of paths that could be followed inland on the Murlough Dunes, and the Lecale Way links with a track that crosses the Downshire Bridge to reach Dundrum. Leaving Dundrum, an old railway trackbed, also known as the Dundrum Coastal Path, can be followed along the shore of Dundrum Inner Bay. Towards the end of this path, roads can be followed up to the castle in the village of Clough. Waymarking is in the form of signposts beside roads, reading Lecale Way, as well as marker posts. There are regular bus services linking Clough with Newcastle.

## THE ROUTE

Leave Newcastle by heading for the beach in front of the Slieve Donard Hotel, turning left to start plodding along the sand and shingle at the foot of a substantial concrete wall. When the tide is out, there is a chance to walk on fairly firm sands, but when the tide is in you may find the higher sand dry, loose and tiring. A very high tide might make the beach walk inadvisable, though further along there are options to cut inland. Timber and boulder banks help to stabilise the dunes at the start of the strand, while timber groins keep the wave-washed sands in check later. Watch carefully while passing the dunes, to spot the Lecale Way heading inland. The route follows a boardwalk across the dunes, reaching a track close to the busy A2 road. Turn right to follow the track beside Dundrum Inner Bay, then turn left to cross Downshire Bridge.

The National Trust owns the Murlough Dunes and has managed them as Ireland's first nature reserve since 1967. Stone Age

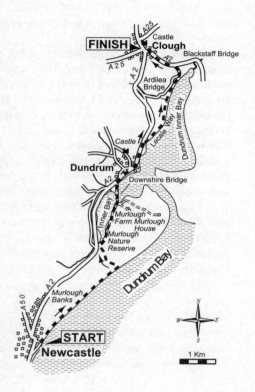

settlements have been discovered beneath the sands, and some of the dunes are so well vegetated that they have become covered in thick, woody scrub. A variety of habitat types includes hazel and buckthorn scrub, a flowery heath, areas of marram grass, sheltered mudflats and a sand-and-shingle foreshore. Dundrum Inner Bay is an important wintering area for Brent geese, waders and ducks, while the open sea supports other ducks and divers, as well as seals. The Murlough Dunes National Nature Reserve supports varied flora, ranging from marram, heather and bracken to rare bee orchid, viper's bugloss, and more common wild pansies and bird's-foot trefoil. The reserve is home to rabbits, foxes and badgers, as well as insects such as moths and butterflies, including the rare marsh fritillary. Birds on the dunes range from skylark and meadow pipit to reed bunting and stonechat, with willow warblers, finches and thrushes also abundant. Shelduck nest in old rabbit burrows, while you may well see ringed plovers on the open beach.

After crossing Downshire Bridge's lovely stone arches, turn right along a short, wooded pathway. The path, like the bridge, is part of an old railway trackbed that once led to Newcastle. The path reaches the busy A2 road close to St Donard's Church in Dundrum. There are places offering food and drink on the way through the village, and there is limited accommodation and a number of bus services if the route is broken at this point. Walking straight through Dundrum, look out for a ruined castle on a wooded hill to the left. The current ruins are of a castle first built by John de Courcy in 1177, but the site has long been fortified and is associated with the mythical Red Branch.

Pass the Dundrum boat park and recreation area, then the Gaelic football ground on the way out of Dundrum. After passing the football ground, turn right to get onto the old railway trackbed again. The National Trust owns this stretch of path, which it has designated the Dundrum Coastal Path. There is a firm, clear path along the top of the embankment, flanked by gorse and brambles. The trackbed gradually pulls away from the busy main road, and there are fine views across the inlet of Dundrum Inner Bay, a popular site for wildfowl and waders. A reedy area is passed and later the track is flanked by a variety of trees. A small tidal lagoon is passed further on, where views are again more open and there is a chance to observe a variety of birds. The track itself

is also notable for its population of badgers. Another wooded stretch leads onwards, and at one point there is a flight of steps leading onto a road. Follow this road away from the shore and turn left along a busier road to continue inland to the village of Clough. You can get food and drink here, or catch a bus, but if you have time to spare be sure to visit the little castle on a grassy 'motte and bailey' just off the main road. The stone castle dates back to the late thirteenth century, but the 'motte and bailey' may have originally carried a wooden structure.

The rare bee orchid.